How
Other Half Loves

A PLAY IN TWO ACTS

By Alan Ayckbourn

SAMUEL FRENCH, INC.

25 WEST 45TH STREET   NEW YORK 10036
7623 SUNSET BOULEVARD   HOLLYWOOD 90046
LONDON   *TORONTO*

HOW THE OTHER HALF LOVES was first presented by Michael Myerberg, Peter Bridge and Eddie Kulukundis in association with Lawrence Shubert Lawrence at the Royale Theatre, N.Y.C., on March 29, 1971. The director was Gene Saks. The original cast was as follows:

CAST
(*In Order of Appearance*)

FIONA FOSTER	*Bernice Massi*
TERESA PHILLIPS	*Sandy Dennis*
FRANK FOSTER	*Phil Silvers*
BOB PHILLIPS	*Richard Mulligan*
WILLIAM DETWEILER	*Tom Aldredge*
MARY DETWEILER	*Jeanne Hepple*

The Time is the Present.

The action of the play takes place in the living rooms of the Fosters and the Phillipses.

ACT ONE

SCENE 1: Thursday morning

SCENE 2: Thursday *AND* Friday night

ACT TWO

SCENE 1: Saturday morning

SCENE 2: Sunday morning

CAST

Frank Foster

Fiona Foster

Bob Phillips

Teresa Phillips

William Detweiler

Mary Detweiler

How the Other Half Loves

ACT ONE

Scene 1

The CURTAIN rises to reveal two living rooms, partially lit. Not a composite setting but with two rooms contained and overlapping in the same area. Only the furnishings themselves, both in color and style, indicate clearly which belongs to which room. The Fosters' (Fiona's *and* Frank's) *is smart period reproduction—a settee, matching armchair and small coffee table, end table and telephone* L. *of sofa, bar* L., *tea cart* U. L., *console table back of sofa. The* Phillips' (Teresa's *and* Bob's) *has rolltop desk and swivel chair* R., *armchair, end table and telephone* C., *rocking chair* L. *of* C., *but more modern, trendy and badly-looked-after. Two doorways. It is early Thursday morning.*

As the curtain rises, Fiona *enters* U. *in her dressing gown. She goes to her window* L. *and draws the curtains. The lights come up on the* Foster *areas and she exits to the kitchen* R. Teresa *enters kitchen,* L., *carrying the Letters to the Editor section of the* New York Times. *She is an intense-looking woman in her early 30s. Since she is in a different room to* Fiona, *she does not acknowledge her presence there in any way. The characters in their different rooms will often pass extremely close but without ever actually touching. She too crosses to bamboo blind on window* R. *and raises it. LIGHTS COME UP on the* Phillips *areas. She switches on her radio. It is a loud news*

program. She sits in swivel chair in front of desk.
FRANK *runs in* U. *wearing his running sweatsuit. He
stops by the timer on his coffee table and jogs up
and down, watching it anxiously. He twice tries to
move timer ahead. It finally rings and he immediately
sits in couch, relieved and relaxed. He then turns on
his portable radio on sofa table to some lively music.*
FIONA *re-enters, crosses down and switches off*
FRANK'S *radio.*

FIONA. I think you're overdoing the jogging, darling.
I'm sure you'll damage yourself one of these days. It's
twenty after. Did you know?
FRANK. That's why I turned on the radio.

(FIONA *exits through* U. *door.*)

TERESA. (*Crossing to her kitchen door and calling.*)
Bob! It's a quarter after. . . . Time to get up! Bob!
(*Gives up after hearing no reply and goes out to kitchen.*)

(FIONA *enters* U. *with mail and newspaper and hands the
paper to* FRANK.)

FIONA. Frank, I'll have to have the car this morning.
. . . (*Back of sofa, opening mail.*)
FRANK. Oh yes?
FIONA. I have so much rushing around to do.
FRANK. Well, you . . . don't have so much rushing
around this morning, do you?
FIONA. I have to rush around every morning, but this
is more hectic than usual. . . .
FRANK. It so happens it's pretty damned inconve-
nient . . .
FIONA. Yes, well, it's inconvenient for both of us. But
I just can't manage without it. . . .
FRANK. Well, as long as that's perfectly clear. (BOB
enters. Early thirties. Very bleary, half-dressed, holding a

Bromo Seltzer. He crosses to PHILLIPS *armchair* C., *sits and drinks the Bromo*.) I mean you're not the only one that has to rush around, you know. I mean, there are times when I'm . . . rushing around. . . . (*Looks up number in Index on end table, then dials phone*.)

FIONA. Yes, well, I'll get us some breakfast. You ought to get dressed. (*Exits kitchen*.)

FRANK. (*Muttering*.) I'm   frequently . . . rushing around. . . .

(PHILLIPS *phone rings*. BOB *answers it*.)

BOB. Hello.

FRANK. Hello. Who's this?

BOB. What?

FRANK. Who am I calling?

BOB. Oh, good morning, Frank. This is Bob Phillips.

FRANK. Good morning, Bob. I've asked everyone to get to the office a little earlier this morning. Tried to find you yesterday. What happened to you? Sneak off a little early, did you?

BOB. Yes, I had—to meet someone—

FRANK. Where? Or shouldn't I ask? (*Laughs.* BOB *imitates his laugh*.) Listen, Bob. Can you make it by a quarter after?

BOB. I'll try.

FRANK. I want the whole team there. Full strength. Right?

BOB. Right. (*Starts to hang up*.)

FRANK. Oh, Bob—

BOB. Yes—

FRANK. What do you know about Detweiler?

BOB. What do I know about what?

FRANK. Detweiler. Bright little fellow from Accounting. Know him?

BOB. Oh. Detweiler. Yes.

FRANK. How do you rate him?

BOB. He's alright.

FRANK. Good man, is he?

BOB. Fine—as far as I know.

FRANK. (*Hangs up.*) Good. Good. Good. (*Takes portable radio, exits* U.) I'm frequently rushing around.

(BOB *looks bewildered, then hangs up.* TERESA *enters from kitchen, engrossed in the paper and sits in rocking chair.*)

BOB. (*After a pause.*) Good morning. (*There is a silence.*) Any coffee?

TERESA. Just made it.

BOB. Good.

TERESA. On the stove—there's another letter from that woman. . . . That's about three this week already. . . .

BOB. On the stove?

TERESA. What?

BOB. The coffee?

TERESA. That's right. Help yourself. . . . This is incredible. She's raised fifteen hundred dollars just in coffee mornings among her friends. Isn't that incredible?

BOB. (*Gets up with Bromo glass and crosses toward kitchen.*) Maybe you ought to do the same thing here. Invite me along. That way I might even get a cup.

(FIONA *enters with a breakfast tray* [*Tray No. 1 (See Prop List*]) *which she puts down and starts to unload on coffee table.*)

TERESA. It's on the stove. . . .

BOB. Fine. (*Exits kitchen.*)

FRANK. (*Offstage.*) Darling . . . darling?

FIONA. Hallo?

FRANK. (*Entering* U.) It seems I have no clean shirts. Is this true? Am I right or am I wrong?

FIONA. Hmmm?

FRANK. (*Crossing* D. *to* L. *of sofa.*) No clean shirts, apparently. I have no clean shirts.

FIONA. Well, darling, if you'd like to run upstairs again and look on the third shelf down, I think you'll find no less than three shirts, all nice and clean and still wrapped in cellophane bags from the laundry. . . .

FRANK. (*Crosses up.*) Third shelf?

FIONA. That's right.

FRANK. (*Turns to* FIONA.) What are they doing on the third shelf?

FIONA. (*Crosses up to* FRANK *with empty tray.*) Presumably lying there waiting for you to put them on.

FRANK. What are they doing on the third shelf? What's wrong with the second shelf . . . ?

FIONA. (*Straightening his jacket.*) Nothing at all as far as I know, dear, but since nineteen fifty-seven your shirts have always been kept on the third shelf down. They have not been kept on the second shelf down since we moved from Allentown. (*Crosses toward kitchen.*)

FRANK. Allentown?

FIONA. We weren't as well off in Allentown, if you remember. You had a smaller wardrobe. . . .

FRANK. I don't know anything about Allentown. . . .

FIONA. (*Going out with the empty tray to kitchen.*) You go and look . . . (*Goes out.*)

FRANK. Why the hell does she have to drag Allentown into the conversation . . . (*Goes out* U., *disgruntled.*)

BOB. (*Entering and standing in kitchen doorway.*) I see you're hanging on with grim nostalgia to this empty cornflake box.

TERESA. Did you get your coffee?

BOB. No. It seems you only made enough for one . . .

TERESA. No, I didn't. . . .

BOB. That was the impression I got from the percolator anyway. I did toy with the idea of chewing the grounds but decided to make some fresh instead.

(FIONA *enters with coffeepot and pours coffee.*)

TERESA. Is Benjamin awake yet?

BOB. Haven't heard him.

TERESA. He's terrific these days. It used to be four o'clock, didn't it?

BOB. So I remember telling you at the time. . . .

TERESA. Oh, I got up now and then, as well.

BOB. (*Starts into kitchen.*) Now and then.

FIONA. (*Going out to kitchen, calling. Leaves coffeepot on coffee table.*) Frank . . . breakfast . . .

TERESA. Did you want some breakfast? Is that what this is all about?

BOB. (*Returning.*) Not if—you're rushed off your feet.

(FIONA *enters with tray No. 2* [*See Prop List*], *sets it on coffee table.*)

TERESA. You know, considering the fact that you rolled in here at two o'clock this morning stinking drunk and I haven't said a word about it . . .

BOB. Till now . . .

TERESA. I haven't said a word about it, I think it's really pretty nervy of you to stand around complaining there isn't any breakfast. . . .

BOB. I'm not complaining.

TERESA. Good.

BOB. (*Going out.*) What the hell have I got to complain about?

FIONA. (*Takes newspaper from sofa and stack table, sets it front of armchair, newspaper on chair, crosses to doors* U.) Frank . . . it's on the table . . .

FRANK. (*Offstage.*) Already . . . ?

(FIONA *shuts doors, goes to phone. Dials.* PHILLIPS *phone rings.* TERESA *answers it.*)

TERESA. Hello. . . .

FIONA. (*Is about to replace the phone when* FRANK *enters through the door.*) . . . eight twenty-eight and twenty seconds. . . . (*Pretends to adjust her watch.*)

TERESA. What? Hello? (FIONA *replaces the receiver.*) Hello? (*After a second she replaces the receiver, puzzled.* TERESA *sits in armchair.*)

FIONA. Eight twenty-eight and twenty seconds . . . (*She crosses to coffee table.*)

FRANK. (*Looks at his watch.*) Is that what it is? Some nut on the radio just said it was eight thirty-three. . . . (*Crosses to armchair and sits.*)

FIONA. (*Crossing with* FRANK'S *breakfast tray and setting it on the stack table.*) Well, they can't both be right. . . .

FRANK. (*Hands her section of the* New York Times.) No. (*Tackles his juice.*)

(FIONA *crosses to sofa, sits, and pours coffee.* BOB *reenters with shirt and tie, carrying his vest, and does an imitation bugle call.*)

BOB. Benjamin is now awake.

TERESA. Is he crying?

BOB. No, just beating on the floor with his wet diaper. . . .

TERESA. He'll be okay for a few minutes. I'd better get you your breakfast. . . .

BOB. (*Crosses and hangs vest on coatrack.*) As I say, don't go out of your way. . . .

TERESA. Oh, shut up. (*Rises.*) Some woman rang up just now. (*Crosses* U. L.)

BOB. Woman?

TERESA. Yes. Told me the time and hung up.

BOB. Oh.

TERESA. Aren't you supposed to call them?

BOB. Usually. Was she abusive . . . make lewd suggestions?

(FRANK *picks up egg and begins to sniff.*)

TERESA. No. She was a couple of minutes fast. . . .

BOB. Nobody I know.

TERESA. I didn't imagine it would be. (*Goes out, and* BOB *finishes buttoning shirt.*)

FIONA. (*Seeing* FRANK *sniff egg.*) It's perfectly fresh.

FRANK. Just make sure. Always make sure first. . . .

FIONA. Yes, I've noticed.

FRANK. (*Tasting.*) Yes. This is fine. Good fresh egg.

(BOB *crosses down to armchair, picks up newspaper, sits.*)

FIONA. Good.

FRANK. (*Eating.*) Very nice. Very nice. . . . (BOB *opens paper revealing cut-out sections, makes disgruntled noise, rises, crosses to desk. Finishes tucking in shirttails and tying tie, then sits, reading newspaper.* FIONA *reads paper.*) Too bad you didn't get home till late last night.

FIONA. Oh? Why's that?

FRANK. Well, with being . . . er . . . well, really no point in it. Just sentimental. (FIONA *looks at him.*) No, no, no . . .

FIONA. Being what?

FRANK. Oh, I don't know why. I always seem to get a little mushy over these things. I don't know why. Women are the ones who're supposed to get mushy, aren't they?

FIONA. Mushy about what, darling?

FRANK. Our wedding anniversary.

FIONA. (*Rises and crosses above to* R. *of* FRANK.) Oh, God.

FRANK. (*Laughing, embarrassed.*) Silly, isn't it?

FIONA. Oh, God.

FRANK. I—er, bought some champagne. You know, the kind you like.

FIONA. You did?

FRANK. Yeah. Drank the whole bottle. Opened it up— let it breathe, tested it for the bouquet . . . and the first thing I know, it's eleven-thirty, and there's not a drop left. (FIONA *crosses to sofa.*) I thought, well, if she walks in now, sees I drank all her special champagne, she'll never forgive me. . . .

FIONA. (*Sits on sofa.*) That's alright. I got held up, I'm afraid.

FRANK. That's what I thought. I thought you were held up. What was it? Another meeting?

FIONA. Umm . . .

(TERESA *enters with sandwich on plate, and dishcloth; she puts dishcloth in the armchair, sandwich on phone table, crosses and sits in rocker and stacks toy on floor.*)

FRANK. No. It couldn't have been a meeting, because your Mrs. Whatshername rang up and said you weren't there and where were you, and I remember saying to her that I thought you must have been held up.

FIONA. Mrs. Who?

FRANK. Whatshername—the one with the mustache. (*Goes back to reading newspaper.*)

FIONA. Oh, God. (*Continues to read newspaper rather angrily.*)

TERESA. I had to get Benjamin up. Put him in his chair. He's peeling the wallpaper in there. I think he's bored. We ought to find something to amuse him—something elastic he can twang on. You know Amy Murchison? Sure, you know Amy Murchison. Amy Murchison gave her little boy an old bra of hers and a couple of tennis balls and that kept him amused for hours. (*Crosses to phone table, picks up plate with sandwich, crosses to BOB.*) I don't like that, though. It's a bit Freudian, isn't it? (*Hands the plate to BOB.*) Here you are.

BOB. What's this?

TERESA. (*Crossing to rocker, picking up stack toy.*) That's your breakfast. I made you a sandwich.

BOB. What sort of sandwich?

TERESA. Peanut butter. (*Crosses to toy box, R. of baby carriage.*)

BOB. (*Staring at it.*) Peanut butter?

TERESA. (*Dropping stack toy in toy box.*) It's all we seem to have.

BOB. You shouldn't have gone to all this trouble, you know.

TERESA. (*Crosses down to him.*) Don't eat the damn thing, then. (*Takes plate from* BOB, *crosses* L., *throws sandwich off plate toward baby carriage, puts plate on phone table, snatches up paper and sits, armchair.*)

FRANK. (*Has finished his egg and holds up toast.*) This toast alright?

FIONA. Perfectly.

FRANK. Seems a little dry. A little dried out, you know.

FIONA. Why don't you dampen it then, darling?

FRANK. (*Doubtfully.*) Um.

BOB. Well, never mind. It was a beautiful thought.

TERESA. Don't you like peanut butter?

BOB. Not round about now I don't.

TERESA. That's funny. Benjamin adores it. . . .

BOB. Does he?

TERESA. Yes. Out of a spoon. He just can't seem to get enough of it.

BOB. Well, obviously I don't take after Benjamin. I'll put it next to the cornflake box. As a memento. (*All read their respective newspapers. Long pause.*) I don't know what we're reading this for. If you've read one newspaper, you've read them all. There's a report in here of this speech—exactly the same speech they reported in yesterday's paper. . . .

TERESA. This is yesterday's paper.

BOB. Yesterday's?

TERESA. I hadn't finished reading it.

BOB. Well, where the hell's today's?

TERESA. I don't know. Outside, probably. (BOB *rises, crosses* L., *front of* TERESA, *going out to kitchen. As he crosses her.*) Would you check and see if Benjamin's alright? Please?

FRANK. Toothbrush is on the fritz.

FIONA. Um?

FRANK. I'll have to take a look at it after breakfast. The electric toothbrush. It's on the fritz.

FIONA. Oh, is it?

FRANK. Battery's weak. Practically dead. Nothing.

FIONA. No?

FRANK. I had to clean my teeth with a washcloth.

FIONA. Your own I hope.

FRANK. Yes. The blue one.

FIONA. That's the one for cleaning the tub!

(FRANK *thoughtfully sucks his teeth.* BOB *enters, imitating danger signal.*)

BOB. Whoop—whoop—whoop!! Benjamin's poured prunes all over his head. . . . Whoop! Whoop! Whoop! (TERESA *leaps up and runs out to kitchen.*) Perhaps he prefers peanut butter. (BOB *follows her out.*)

FRANK. Where did you finally go then?

FIONA. When?

FRANK. Last night?

FIONA. Oh, I got held up. . . .

FRANK. Oh. (*Pause.*) I see. Doesn't matter.

FIONA. It's no secret. There's no secret about it.

FRANK. Isn't there?

FIONA. No secret at all.

FRANK. Good.

FIONA. More coffee?

FRANK. No, thank you.

(BOB *enters, laughing, crosses and sits in rocker.* TERESA *comes pounding on after him, crosses to front door, gets milk and newspaper from outside.*)

TERESA. I don't know what you think is so damn funny.

BOB. I like the way he looks in prunes. . . .

TERESA. (*Sourly.*) Oh ha-ha . . . (*Hands* BOB *newspaper.*) You're a great help. A great help, aren't you? (*Goes out to kitchen.*)

(FIONA *rises and crosses to* FRANK *to clear breakfast tray.*)

FRANK. Mustn't forget to give you your present.

FIONA. Present?

FRANK. Your anniversary present. Mustn't forget to give it to you before I go.

FIONA. (*Takes tray, crosses* U. R.) There's no need to rub it in, darling.

FRANK. What? Oh. I didn't intend to. I didn't mean to rub it in.

FIONA. Good.

FRANK. Good Lord, no.

(FIONA *goes out, puts tray off* R.)

TERESA. (*Enters, with washcloth, crosses to phone table, picks up plate.*) Where the hell were you last night, anyway?

BOB. Me?

TERESA. Where were you? (*Crosses into kitchen, puts plate down on cabinet shelf.*)

(FIONA *enters, crosses to sofa, sits and reads paper.*)

BOB. That's a funny question.

TERESA. No, I'm sick of this. (*Crosses to* BOB.) Other husbands tell their wives where they go. They don't just disappear and come rolling in at two o'clock in the morning. Other husbands are more considerate. I mean here I am stuck here with Benjamin and you're out having fun and God knows what else, and here I am stuck here.

BOB. (*Rises, puts paper down and crosses above chair, takes vest from coatrack, puts it on.*) What has this got to do with anything?

TERESA. (*Follows* BOB.) He's your child as much as he is mine.

BOB. I believe you.

TERESA. Well, where were you? I want to know. Where were you?

(FIONA *crosses to bar, picks up the* TV Guide.)

BOB. (*Crosses to desk; indignant.*) Out.

TERESA. Just out?

BOB. That's right.

TERESA. What doing?

BOB. Drinking, talking . . .

TERESA. Who with?

BOB. (*Crosses* D. R.) Why do you want to know?

TERESA. Because I'm not an idiot, you know. I'm not a complete idiot. I mean I'd be very stupid indeed if I didn't notice . . . (*A crash off.*) Benjamin!—If I didn't notice certain things that are going on in this house. . . . (*Another crash.*) Benjamin! All right, just consider the fact that I am not finished with you. . . . (*Hurrying off.*) Benjamin, you cut that out . . . right now! (*Goes out.*)

FRANK. (*Rising.*) I think I'll get it for you, anyway. The present . . . (*Goes out.*)

FIONA. (*Annoyed, crosses with* TV Guide *and sits in armchair.*) Oh. . . .

TERESA. (*Returning with a spoon and a washcloth, crosses to* BOB.) I caught him trying to swallow this spoon.

BOB. Really?

TERESA. He could have choked. Easily.

BOB. I think he'd have stood a good chance.

TERESA. (*Crosses to* D. L. *of* C.) You don't care. You don't care at all, do you? You don't care. You don't care about me, you don't care about Benjamin. . . . You just don't care.

(*Pause.*)

BOB. What's the matter with you?

TERESA. (*More subdued.*) I don't think I can cope. I've just about had it and I don't think I can cope, anymore.

BOB. You do alright.

TERESA. The house is a mess. I'm in a mess. Benjamin's covered with prunes. . . . (*Crosses* U. C.) Everything's terrible. (*Crosses* D. L.) Then I read the papers and I feel more useless. Do you know that woman who raised that fifteen hundred dollars? (*Crosses to* BOB.) She's got three children. . . .

BOB. So what? (*Crosses to kitchen door.*) She's probably got fifteen in help . . .

TERESA. (*Crosses* U. *between the two chairs.*) Three children. Here's me with one and I can't cope. *And* she writes letters. . . .

BOB. You write letters . . .

TERESA. Yes, but nobody ever publishes mine though. I mean there must be something I can do. Something worthwhile. Instead of just sitting here, on my ass, like a . . . cow, or something. (*Pause.*) You're never here.

BOB. I'm always here . . . mostly.

TERESA. Not when I need you, you're not. Not when I want to talk. (*Crosses* U. *and leans against door* U.)

(BOB *exits to kitchen.*)

FRANK. (*Re-entering* U. *with a small parcel done up with ribbon.*) Here we are. (*Crosses down to* R. *of* FIONA.) Open your mouth, close your eyes, prepare yourself for a big surprise. (*Hands* FIONA *the present.*)

FIONA. Oh. Thank you, darling. (*Puts present on table, looks at* TV Guide.)

FRANK. Open it up. Open it up. (*Crosses* L. *of chair.*)

FIONA. Oh, alright. You do realize, I've completely forgotten to get you anything, don't you?

FRANK. Yes. That's alright. That's alright.

(FIONA *starts to open parcel.*)

TERESA. There must be someone I can help.

BOB. (*Off.*) Who?

TERESA. I don't know. (*Crosses to desk.*) Anyone.

FIONA. (*Pulls out a bottle of perfume from the parcel.*) Oh. How nice. How very nice. Thank you, darling. Very thoughtful.

FRANK. That's the kind you like, isn't it?

FIONA. No. Not really.

FRANK. Oh. (*Pause.*) Oh, I see.

FIONA. No, I don't usually wear this one, dear. (TERESA *sits at desk.*) What a lovely pretty bottle, though, isn't it?

FRANK. Well, I can exchange it.

FIONA. (*Rises and crosses* U. R. *with wrappings and box.*) No, it's alright, darling. There's no need to bother. (*Turning to* FRANK.) I'll just wear it round the house. That sort of thing. (*Crosses to kitchen with coffeepot and one cup, re-enters and goes to sofa table.*)

FRANK. (*Crossing up.*) Had some time getting that. You see I couldn't remember the name. So I had this girl in the store opening up bottles . . . (*Crosses to platform.*) . . . letting me smell each one. Then she started putting it all over herself so I could smell her. Well, I got a little embarrassed, standing there in the middle of this big store, smelling away at her like mad. People were starting to stare. Because there I was sniffing her all over. They must have thought I had some kind of fetish . . . (*Goes out.*)

FIONA. Thank you, darling. It was a lovely thought.

BOB. (*Entering, crosses to* D. C.) As a matter of fact . . .

TERESA. (*Rises and crosses* C.) What?

BOB. (*At* C.) Do you know who I was out with last night?

TERESA. Who?

BOB. William.

TERESA. William who?

BOB. (*Crossing* U.) William Detweiler . . .

TERESA. William Detweiler?—Oh him.—Yes.—Works in your office, doesn't he?

BOB. (*Crosses* U.) No. Same firm but different department.

TERESA. Oh, I see.

BOB. Yes, I was out with him.

TERESA. What doing?

BOB. Oh, you know. Drinking. Talking.

TERESA. I didn't know William Detweiler was a friend of yours?

BOB. Well, no, he's not really. We talk, now and then.

TERESA. Oh. I've only met him once, haven't I? Wasn't he at that awful office party?

BOB. That's right.

TERESA. (*Kneels in armchair.*) With his wife—what's her name?

BOB. Mary.

TERESA. That's it. I remember they were awfully boring, weren't they? What did you want to ask him out for?

BOB. He asked me really. . . .

TERESA. I cannot imagine you and William Detweiler had much in common.

BOB. Well—we talked shop . . . mostly.

TERESA. Till two in the morning?

BOB. (*Crosses* R.) That and . . . other things.

TERESA. I wish you'd talk to me till two in the morning, and other things. . . . What else did you talk about, then? Do you know what I think? I think you're making all this up. I can't believe you were out with William Detweiler all that time. . . .

BOB. Well, where else do you think I was, then?

TERESA. I dread to think!

FRANK. (*Off.*) Darling!—Crisis!—We're out of bathroom stationery!

FIONA. (*Coming in, with an enormous sigh.*) Oh, dear. (*Calling.*) Just a minute. (*Goes out* U. *door.*)

BOB. (*Crosses to* R. *of* TERESA.) No. If you must know . . . William's a bit upset. . . .

TERESA. Why?

BOB. Well, it's very complicated . . . but . . . he thinks his wife is having an affair . . .

TERESA. Mary?

BOB. That's what he thinks.

TERESA. That sounds very unlikely. If I remember Mary.

Bob. Oh, I don't know, though. . . .

Teresa. She doesn't seem to be the type. She's a . . . very twitchy girl. I can't imagine anyone running after Mary Detweiler. . . .

Bob. She's not bad-looking, at all. . . .

Teresa. Oh . . .

Bob. Quite attractive as a matter of fact . . . to a man.

Teresa. Oh, really?

Bob. Not bad at all.

Teresa. Does she turn you on?

Bob. Well, no—not personally. But I know a lot of people she does. (*Crosses to kitchen door.*)

Teresa. Who's she having this thing with, then?

Bob. William doesn't know. It's all very secret, you mustn't say anything. He was very broken up about it, though.

Teresa. I'm sorry.—Oh, dear. They haven't got any children, have they?

Bob. No. He's a great planner, William.

Teresa. Oh. Did you advise him?

Bob. (*In kitchen door.*) Yes, I told him it would probably blow over.

Teresa. See! That's what you usually do.

Bob. What else could I say?

Teresa. (*Crosses to* Bob.) Well, sometimes things don't. Unless you do something positive. Sometimes you really have to do something. It isn't enough just to say— oh, Benjamin's ill, it'll blow over . . . the house is on fire, it'll blow over. Sometimes it isn't enough just to sit back.

Bob. And what was I supposed to have done then?

Teresa. He wanted advice. He came to you—God knows why—for advice.

Bob. You can't advise anyone in those circumstances.

Teresa. Yes, you could. You could have. If you'd been a trained marriage counselor you could have. (Fiona *enters. Goes to phone, dials.* Bob *starts out.* Teresa *fol-*

lows.) I mean, you could have at least told him to talk to the poor woman. It may be that there're all sorts of things that with a talk they could clear the whole thing up.

(PHILLIPS *PHONE RINGS.* BOB *enters fully dressed except for shoes and carrying one brown loafer. He sits and answers phone.*)

BOB. Hello.

FIONA. Hello.

FRANK. (*Entering with toothbrush.*) Sweetheart . . .

FIONA. (*Into phone.*) Yes. . . . Yes. . . . Just a rinse and set would be lovely. . . .

FRANK. Oh, I'm sorry. I didn't know you were on the phone.

FIONA. Darling, I wonder would you be a lamb and get the car out into the driveway for me? I always snag my stockings or something.

FRANK. Well, I was just looking for the screwdriver.

FIONA. Bless you, darling. . . . Hello, yes, yes. . . .

BOB. Has he gone?

FIONA. (*As* FRANK *goes.*) Just about. Yes. Can you talk?

BOB. Yes. Just for a minute, though. I'm on my way out.

FIONA. Listen, do you know what last night was?

BOB. Marvelous.

FIONA. It was my wedding anniversary, for God's sake.

BOB. Oh, really?—Congratulations.

FIONA. Oh, yes, it's a scream. I feel terrible about it.

TERESA. (*Entering suddenly.*) Bob!

BOB. Yes?

FIONA. What?

TERESA. Get up.

BOB. (*Rises.*) Listen, old buddy, I would just divide the whole figure by two-thirds. . . .

TERESA. (*Takes washcloth from chair.*) You were sitting on the washcloth.

FIONA. Is she there?
BOB. Yes.

(FIONA *sits sofa.*)

TERESA. You would not believe what that child of yours has done with an entire jar of honey. (*Goes out. BOB sits as FIONA rises.*)
BOB. —You were saying . . .
FIONA. Listen, the point is, Frank's getting very curious about where I was last night.
BOB. That's funny. Same thing here.
FIONA. What do I tell him?
BOB. You were with a friend.
FIONA. No. He knows practically everyone, it's too risky. . . .
BOB. Look, I've got to go in a second. . . .
FIONA. You haven't told me what I'm going to say. . . .
BOB. I don't know.
FIONA. What did you tell Terry, then?
BOB. That I ran into someone.
FIONA. Who?
BOB. William Detweiler.
FIONA. William who?
BOB. Detweiler. He works in the Accounts Department at the office. Anyway, he's married to Mary Detweiler. . . .
FIONA. (*Sits.*) Oh, yes, I remember them. What made you think of them?
BOB. They're safe, obscure. . . . Anyway, it's the first name that popped into my head.
FIONA. Go on. What?
BOB. Their marriage is breaking up.
FIONA. Really? I didn't know.
BOB. No! Not really, That's just the story. But since it's all very hush, hush nobody's to say a word. . . .
FIONA. You mean she fell for a line like that?

BOB. Why not?

TERESA. (*Off.*) Bob . . . come and look at this . . .

BOB. Coming!—Look, I've got to go. . . . Say what you like. . . . (*Hangs up.*)

FIONA. But what about . . . ?

(BOB *has hung up.*)

TERESA. (*Off.*) Bob . . .

FIONA. Bob—

BOB. (*Going off.*) What?

FRANK. (*Entering with toothbrush.*) What?

FIONA. (*Rises, putting phone on phone table.*) Oh, have you taken the car out?

FRANK. It's still in the driveway. You never did put it away last night.

FIONA. Oh. How silly of me.

FRANK. As a matter of fact, only two wheels are in the driveway, the other two are on the front lawn.

FIONA. (*Crosses R. to sofa table.*) You must go. . . .

FRANK. Yes. I was . . . Have you seen that screw-driver?

FIONA. Screwdriver?

FRANK. Screwdriver. (*Crosses to R. of* FIONA, *searching for screwdriver.*) You know, for screwing things. I've got to take the end off this toothbrush to get at the batteries.

FIONA. You don't want to do that now. . . .

FRANK. Might as well do it now as later. I don't want to spend the whole evening sitting in the bathroom with a screwdriver. Did you put it somewhere?

FIONA. Have you tried the toolbox?

FRANK. Toolbox?

FIONA. In the laundry room.

FRANK. Oh, that toolbox. Is that where you put it? I wondered where it went to. (BOB *enters with same brown shoe, and clutching a blue folder. He crosses to desk, looking for his other shoe.*) The other day I was looking for the hammer. (*Goes out.*)

FIONA. (*Calling.*) You'll have to hurry. (*Exits* U.)
TERESA. (*Off.*) Bob . . .
BOB. What is it?

(TERESA *enters and crosses to* D. C.)

TERESA. Bob . . . don't you think I'm right, that if William and Mary could just get together . . .
BOB. (*Crosses to* TERESA.) Look, Terry, I'm late for a meeting. Forget about William and Mary and find my shoe. . . .
TERESA. I haven't had it. . . .
BOB. There's nothing we can do about them, you're not supposed to know, anyway. . . .
TERESA. What kind of a shoe?
BOB. The same as this one. Only pointing the other way. . . .
TERESA. (*Going off to kitchen.*) I don't know why you think I'm the one that should have it.
BOB. (*Crosses* R. *and up to toy box and back to* C.) I think you might have had it for the same reason you had this file of last year's estimated growth figures which I just found in the bread box. . . . If you'd stop worrying a minute about other people and start organizing this place you'd be making a very valuable contribution to world peace . . .
TERESA. (*Entering and crossing to* BOB.) Stop fussing. It's alright, I've found it. (*Holds out a black shoe and then notices that* BOB *is holding a brown one.*) Oh. . . .
BOB. Well, it might be a novelty. . . .
TERESA. (*Crosses up to baby carriage, then down to desk.*) I'm sorry. I don't know where it is. . . .
BOB. Never mind. Maybe if I walk sideways no one will notice.

(BOB *and* TERESA *search.* FIONA *re-enters with coat, umbrella and hat, and places them on chair.*)

FRANK. (*Entering from kitchen with box and crossing to* FIONA.) Not in here. No screwdriver in here.

FIONA. I didn't imagine there would be, darling.

FRANK. You distinctly said . . .

(TERESA *sits, desk chair, facing front,* BOB *searches in and under desk.*)

FIONA. (*Starts out to kitchen.*) Those are the shoe brushes.

FRANK. Shoe brushes. What are they doing in my toolbox?

FIONA. (*Exiting to kitchen.*) Come in here and I'll show you.

FRANK. (*Following her.*) What are shoe brushes doing in my toolbox?

BOB. (*Discovering the missing shoe in the wastebasket, holds it up.*) What's this then?

TERESA. Well, there it is.

BOB. How did it get in there, for crying out loud?

TERESA. Oh, I think I gave it to Benjamin to play with last night. . . .

BOB. Well, for God's sake, why don't you buy him some toys? Why must he play with my clothing? (BOB *puts foot into shoe, squeezing sound is heard. He reacts, then pulls squeeze toy from shoe.*) What's this? (*Holds it up.*)

TERESA. Oh, that's his tomato. He loves playing grocery store with your shoes. . . .

BOB. (*Savagely.*) Tell him to buy his own goddamn shoes. (*Crosses to coatrack, starts to put on shoe.*)

TERESA. Honestly, the way you talk about him, sometimes, terrifies me. You're supposed to be his father. . . .

BOB. (*Still putting on shoe.*) Terry. I'm late. I am very late. Now do me a favor. During the day, just go around very slowly and try and straighten up this dump, will you?

TERESA. Oh, that's lovely. (BOB *crosses to* TERESA, *taking money out of his pocket.*) Here I am, stuck in this house day after day with that child. . . .

BOB. (*Handing* TERESA *money.*) And here is twenty dollars. Twenty whole dollars. Now go mad. Go out to

the nearest delicatessen and try buying some food.
(*Crosses back to coatrack and takes coat and attaché
case.*) Not just jars of peanut butter . . . but real
food. . . .

TERESA. Oh go on, clear out. . . .

BOB. And another thing, wash that child, will you?
(*Opens door.*) He's got enough food plastered on his face
to feed a family of four. (*Exits.*)

TERESA. (*Rises, crosses to door, carrying phone book,
opens door and yells out.*) That's right! Go on, walk out.
You're no help, you're no help at all, are you? (*Crosses
back to desk, sits, goes through phonebook until she finds
number, tears out page, crosses to phone, sits armchair,
puts phone in lap and dials.* FIONA *enters and crosses to
the phone, calls* TERESA, *gets a busy signal, sighs and
hangs up, crosses and sits on arm of Foster chair, picks
up coat, hat.*) Hello . . . is this Mary Detweiler? This is
Teresa Phillips. . . . I don't know if you'll remember me,
but . . . Yes, that's right, yes. Look, Mary, I know this
is sort of out of the blue, but Bob and I were wondering
if you and your husband would like to come over for
dinner some night. . . . Well, what about tonight? Oh,
are you? Well, what about tomorrow then? You're free?
Wonderful. Let's make it tomorrow—Friday— I don't
care. What is good for you. (FRANK *enters kitchen, fid-
dling with screwdriver and toothbrush crosses to sofa
table.*) —eight o'clock. Yes. Yes. So am I. Good-bye.

FIONA. Have you done it?

FRANK. Not yet. You have to be careful with these
things or you can give yourself a nice shock. (*The toothbrush flies apart.*) Ah.

FIONA. Good work, dear.

FRANK. No, it came apart. Typical. (*Puts screwdriver
in his outside breast pocket—crosses to* FIONA *with toothbrush. She picks up coat.*) Typical modern workmanship.
Came apart in my hands.

FIONA. Darling, you've unscrewed the wrong end. The
batteries go in there. (*Puts his coat on him.*)

(TERESA *gets up from the chair and exits to kitchen.*)

FRANK. Useless. Absolutely useless. (*As* FIONA *hands him the articles.*) Hat, umbrella. (*Toothbrush comes out through coat sleeve.*) Toothbrush.

FIONA. You'll have to hurry.

FRANK. I want to drop this off at the garage. Get them to take a look at it. Something defective here.

FIONA. Leave that now, dear. Have you got your brief-case?

FRANK. (*Peering at breakfast table.*) Yes, it's in the— (*Picking up the perfume.*) If you told me the name of your stuff, I'd make them exchange it.

FIONA. (*Takes perfume, puts it back on table.*) Now, do hurry. . . .

FRANK. Yes. (*Looking at his watch.*) Good God, yes. . . . Where the hell is my—er . . . (*Picks up* TV Guide.)

FIONA. In the hall. (*Starts out.*)

FRANK. Good show on television last night, by the way. You'd have loved it. . . .

FIONA. (*Off.*) I'll get your briefcase.

FRANK. (*Calling after her.*) It was about this fella who . . . there were two of them at first, but one had to drop out with a pulled muscle. Anyway, this other guy made a go of it alone. Damn near made it too. . . .

FIONA. (*Returning with briefcase, to his left.*) Here you are. . . .

FRANK. . . . No, that's right. There were *three* of them in the beginning. One had the pulled muscle and the other one had—er . . . what the hell happened to the other one? I know there was only one left at the end. . . . (FIONA *puts* TV Guide *on table.*) Oh, he died. That's it.

FIONA. Off you go. (*Turning him and propelling him to door.*) Off you go now.

FRANK. He died, leaving the other fellow to make a go of it alone.

FIONA. Bye-bye. (*Hands him his briefcase.*)

FRANK. Yes—bye-bye, darling. Nice to have seen you. (*Exits through* R. *double door and* FIONA *closes it, then turns to the front.* FRANK *returns immediately through* L. *double door.*) Say, whatever happened to you last night? You never did tell me, did you?

FIONA. (*Crosses* U. C.) Didn't I?

FRANK. No. I was a little confused, because I thought I heard you say earlier that you were going to that meeting, but then this Mrs.—er—thing calls up and says you haven't been there so I got a little worried . . .

FIONA. (*Crosses and puts paper off sofa, then crosses to sofa table and puts paper on it.*) No, well, actually . . . I decided to skip that boring meeting for once and hurry home. I was on my way, and then . . . who should I run into but Mary Detweiler . . .

FRANK. *Mary* Detweiler? Who's *Mary* Detweiler?

FIONA. (*Crosses to coffee table.*) She's William Detweiler's wife, darling. Isn't he with your company?

FRANK. Yes . . . he is. I didn't know you were friendly with her.

FIONA. Well, we hardly . . . I mean, hardly at all. (*Crosses out with tray No. 2.*) Just one of those dreary office parties, that's the only time . . . (*Crosses* D. R. *to coffee table, picks up cup and saucer.*)

FRANK. (*Crosses* D. *between the chairs.*) Well, you certainly made a night of it, I must say.

FIONA. (*Crosses* U. *between* PHILLIPS *chair and sofa.*) Yes, well, the point is . . . Now this is terribly secret, darling, you mustn't breathe a word to anyone . . .

FRANK. What is?

FIONA. (*Steps in toward* FRANK.) Promise?

FRANK. Of course. What?

FIONA. Well, Mary is terribly upset.

FRANK. Why?

FIONA. I'm just telling you.

FRANK. I'm sorry, dear.

FIONA. Putting it all in the crudest possible terms . . .

she's pretty sure that William has another woman. (*Crosses* u.)

FRANK. Another one?

FIONA. (*As to a child.*) An affair, darling. A love affair.

FRANK. You're kidding. You're pulling my leg. For heaven's sake. Detweiler?

FIONA. Yes.

FRANK. (*Sitting armchair.*) Good grief. This is shattering . . . appalling.

FIONA. Yes, well, Mary was very upset, of course. And for some reason she chose to pour it all out to me, but you mustn't say a word, dear.

FRANK. No, of course not. Well, I've got to say, I'm absolutely appalled by this. . . .

FIONA. (*Crosses above sofa.*) Yes. Of course, we hardly know them . . . but all the same . . .

FRANK. That's beside the point. Whether we know them or not's beside the point.

FIONA. It is? Why?

FRANK. Well. There's something you don't know. I didn't tell you. Detweiler's coming into my department.

FIONA. (*Blankly.*) Oh, is he?

FRANK. We're expanding. So he's coming with us. It's a key job. He won't be much good to us if he's doing all this carrying on. Is this wife of his sure of her facts?

FIONA. Well, I suppose she is, yes. Of course she could possibly be wrong. . . .

FRANK. But, if she's upset enough to talk to a comparative stranger till God knows when in the morning . . .

FIONA. (*Crosses to coffee table, picks up coffeepot.*) Tell me, does Bob Phillips know about this appointment?

FRANK. Bob Phillips? No. Why?

FIONA. (*Crosses* u., *puts pot on sofa table.*) Well, I thought, being that he's in your department . . . ?

FRANK. Oh, no, no, no. You can't release these things prematurely. It's a top level decision. I'm announcing it this morning. (*Seeing the toothbrush on the table, picks it up.*) I thought I had this with me. Have we got of these things? (*Replaces toothbrush.*) My God, this is going to be embarrassing tonight, isn't it? (*Crosses D.*)

FIONA. (*Crossing D. C.*) What is?

FRANK. (*Turns to FIONA.*) I mean I had no idea at the time . . .

FIONA. What?

FRANK. That the Detweilers . . . Oh, now I know, I know, I know. . . . Now I know. I know what it was I was thinking last night when you didn't get back. I remember thinking— (*Crosses away and back.*) Son of a gun . . . I remember thinking, I mustn't forget. I remember thinking . . .

FIONA. (*Simultaneously as last line.*) Darling, what are you trying to say?

FRANK. I've invited the Detweilers to dinner.

FIONA. Tonight?

FRANK. Yes.

FIONA. (*Crosses to above sofa table.*) Oh, that's out of the question. . . .

FRANK. (*Crossing U.*) You're not going out again, are you?

FIONA. (*Turns to FRANK.*) Yes, I may be. . . .

FRANK. Well, can't you cancel it? Where are you going?

FIONA. . . . Um . . . nowhere, no. I'm not going out. (*Turns away.*)

FRANK. Oh, that's fine. Fine. I'm sure you'll manage. Sure you will. . . . Do I need a coat?

FIONA. You've got one on.

FRANK. (*Exiting.*) Yes, right. Dinner at eight— (*Goes out and closes door.*)

FIONA. (*Dully.*) 'Bye. (*Crosses to stack table, picks up toothbrush and TV Guide, crosses to sofa table, puts Guide on sofa table, goes to phone and dials. After three digits, she looks at toothbrush still in her hand and drops it in the wastebasket, finishes dialing, picks up phone, sits on sofa. PHILLIPS phone rings, and on second ring FRANK enters.* FIONA *turns and hides phone under sofa cushion, picks up letter from sofa table and starts to read.*)

FRANK. Ah! (*Points somewhat accusingly at* FIONA.)

FIONA. What's that, darling?

FRANK. The toothbrush.

FIONA. Mmm?

FRANK. (*Crosses down.*) Forgot the toothbrush, didn't I? Where did it go?

FIONA. (*Points at wastebasket.*) In the wastebasket. I'm afraid I threw it away.

(TERESA *enters, crosses to ringing phone.*)

FRANK. (*Holding up basket and peering in.*) Ah! (*Takes out the toothbrush.*) Caught you this time.

TERESA. (*Answers the phone.*) Hello. . . .

FRANK. (*Crosses* R.) Now then, where's the—er . . .

FIONA. What's the matter, dear?

TERESA. Hello?

FRANK. Can't seem to . . . see it . . . anywhere. . . .

FIONA. What?

(FRANK *doesn't reply but wanders round peering under furniture, etc.*)

TERESA. Hello, who is this?

FIONA. What are you looking for?

FRANK. The—thingummyjig. (*Gestures vaguely. They search.*)

TERESA. Hello. Look . . . If you're one of those callers . . . You'd better hang up right now.

FRANK. (*Goes into kitchen.*) You didn't throw that away, too, did you?

FIONA. (*Follows him.*) Throw what away?

TERESA. I'm warning you, my husband is very strong. He's a professional wrestler. He has a very bad temper. And we also have dogs. . . . (FRANK *enters from the kitchen to above sofa.*) Enormous dogs . . .

FIONA. (*Off.*) Darling, what are we looking for?

FRANK. (*Lifts sofa cushion, finds phone, picks it up, absently.*) Screwdriver.

TERESA. And you too! (*Goes out.*)

FRANK. (*Replaces the receiver and finds the screwdriver in his breast pocket.*) Ah! it's alright, darling, I've got it. (*Crosses to U. doors.*) Don't panic. Got it.

FIONA. (*Returns from kitchen.*) Good-bye, darling. Bye-bye now.

FRANK. Did I tell you?—Dinner at eight. 'Bye. (*Exits.*)

(FIONA *crosses to armchair.* TERESA *enters with glass of milk, crosses and picks up sandwich she had thrown U.* TERESA *crosses to desk and sits. During this* FIONA *crosses with stack table and puts it away.* FIONA *and* TERESA *pick up telephone pads and pencils.*)

FIONA. Dinner at eight. Mmm.

TERESA. Mmm.

FIONA. (*Thoughtfully.*) Avocado.

TERESA. (*Crosses L. to rocker and sits.*) Can of chicken broth.

FIONA. Veal.

TERESA. Chopped chuck.

FIONA. Endives.

TERESA. Brussels sprouts.

FIONA. Sour cream.

TERESA. Frozen french fries.

FIONA. Zabaglione.

TERESA. Jello.

FIONA. Chablis.

TERESA. Booze!

(*They both rise.* TERESA *crosses U. L.,* FIONA *crosses U. R. of C.*)

BOTH. Coffee.

CURTAIN

ACT ONE

SCENE 2

The same. Evening. FIONA, L., *and* TERESA, U., *are simultaneously laying their own particular section of the table. Obviously,* FIONA'S *banquet is on a far grander scale than* TERESA'S *cozy supper.* FIONA *crosses* R. *in front of table with two napkins, plates, silverware settings and placemats, and sets Frank and Mary places, folding napkins so they stand up.* TERESA *sets William's and Mary's and her places.* FIONA *crosses back to serving cart, sets her own and William's places, while* TERESA *sets Bob's place, tearing towels off paper towel roll and puts them on table. As* TERESA *places fourth paper towel at William's setting—*

FRANK. (*Off.*) Darling . . .

BOB. (*Entering.*) Terry . . .

FIONA. In here, dear.

TERESA. Hello. (*Crosses to* BOB *and kisses him.*)

FRANK. (*Entering* U. *with wet umbrella and hat and coat.*) Hello, darling.

FIONA. (*Without looking up.*) Hello.

FRANK. Rotten night, you know. Absolutely rotten. (*Takes off coat and hat, exits.*)

TERESA. (*She and* BOB *break away from kiss.*) How are you?

BOB. (*Puts attaché case down.*) Thank God it's Friday. That's all I can say.

TERESA. Bet I know what you'd like.

BOB. What?

TERESA. An ice cold beer in a specially chilled glass.

BOB. (*Puzzled.*) Yes . . . ? (TERESA *takes his hand, and they go into kitchen.*)

FRANK. (*Entering, crosses to* FIONA *and kisses her on the cheek.*) Pouring. Absolutely pouring. (*Crosses to bar.*)

FIONA. Make me a drink, will you, dear? I'm dying for one. You did say eight o'clock, didn't you?

FRANK. —Er, more or less, I think.

FIONA. I mean if they arrive any earlier, I'm just not going to be ready, that's all.

FRANK. (*Pouring drinks at the sideboard.*) Terrific downpour tonight. Terrific.

FIONA. I know. And that back drain's overflowing again, as a result.

FRANK. Is it? Is it? Oh well, I'll get out there and give it a few pokes with the coat hanger.

FIONA. I don't think your little pokes are very effective, darling. (FRANK *crosses to* FIONA.) Last time I looked, it was nearly up to the window sill.

FRANK. Here we are. (*Hands* FIONA *a drink.*)

FIONA. Thank you, darling. (*Drinks.*) Mmm. Lovely. (*Sitting.*) You know, I don't know how I got through today—I really don't. (FRANK *sits.*) Do me a favor, dear. If you're going to spring these surprise dinner parties on me, please don't do it on a Thursday again. It's one of my busiest days.

FRANK. Well, you're pretty busy every day. What's so special about Thursday?

FIONA. Well, for one thing, the Planned Motherhood Committee.

FRANK. Oh, yes. I forgot they planned on Thursdays.

FIONA. Anyway, I hope these people are going to be worth it.

FRANK. Oh, I think so. He's a . . . he's a nice enough fellow. And you know her, of course.

FIONA. Do I? Oh!—yes—only slightly. And remember, dear, we're not going to mention anything about that, are we?

FRANK. Mmmm?

FIONA. About William and—er . . .

FRANK. Oh, God, no. I'd strongly advise you not to mention it. . . .

FIONA. Fine. No confrontations, then?

(Bob *enters from kitchen, no jacket and tie undone, and crosses to* R. *of table. He sees the table laid.*)

FRANK. No need. (*They sit drinking.*)

BOB. Terry!

TERESA. (*Off.*) Coming. (*Enters with four knives.*)

BOB. What's all this for?

TERESA. (*Picks up wooden tray.*) Oh. I'll tell you. In a second. (*Goes into kitchen.*)

BOB. (*Glaring at the table.*) If you've asked your mother over . . .

FRANK. No, he's a decent enough fellow. Detweiler. Has a peculiar hobby, though. Don't know what it is. Wears boots for it. Keeps them on top of his filing cabinet.

BOB. Terry. Who is coming?

TERESA. (*Off.*) Wait.

FRANK. Great big boots. Don't know what he uses them for. (TERESA *enters.*) But it isn't mountain climbing, I'll tell you that.

TERESA. (*Handing* BOB *a mug of tea.*) Here you are. The sugar's in it.

BOB. What happened to the beer?

TERESA. (*Crosses and puts* BOB's *knife down.*) We don't have any.

BOB. (*Sets cup of tea on table.*) And who have you invited for dinner tonight?

TERESA. (*Crosses* U., *puts knives down for herself and the Detweilers.*) I wish you wouldn't shout. I just got Benjamin off to sleep.

BOB. (*Quietly.*) I am asking you . . . who?

(TERESA *crosses to kitchen door.*)

FRANK. And it's not hiking, either. . . .

TERESA. (*Turns to* BOB.) Well . . . the Detweilers, actually. (*Exits.*)

BOB. (*Turns away, then turns to kitchen door, pulls*

the ends of his tie across his throat in a choking gesture, crosses up, leans against kitchen door.) I see.

FRANK. I'll tell you something else. (*Rises, crosses R. above sofa.*) Whatever he does in those boots, he doesn't take his wife. I know that. Goes off on his own. Which either means that it's dangerous . . . (TERESA *enters, puts down her spoon and Detweilers'.*) or else . . . or else it's tied up with this other business. (*Crosses above sofa to L. of sofa.*)

BOB. And what exactly do you intend to do? Settle their marriage over dinner?

TERESA. Certainly not.

BOB. Well?

TERESA. (*Crosses down and puts down BOB's spoon, crosses up into kitchen.*) If friends need help . . .

BOB. They'll ask for it. Exactly. When did you decide to invite them over here?

TERESA. Yesterday morning. After you told me.

BOB. I see. And now we have to sit through a whole evening of them. We have a whole goddamn boring evening ahead of us . . . (*Crossing R.*) just because you have nothing better to do with your time.

TERESA. (*Enters with forks and puts down hers and the Detweilers'.*) I have plenty of other . . .

BOB. (*At door.*) Then mind your own business.

TERESA. If you had an ounce of sensitivity . . . (*Crossing down and putting BOB's fork down.*)

BOB. I'm sensitive enough to know when people want to be left alone.

TERESA. (*Crosses to kitchen door.*) Well. It's too late now. They're coming. (*Goes into kitchen.*)

FRANK. Do you think this is a possibility? He uses those boots to tramp off and see this other woman. Maybe she lives in a marsh, or something. Which explains why he keeps them in his office. Doesn't want his wife to see them. You see?

(TERESA *enters with soupspoons and bottle of wine, puts*

wine on table, sets down hers and Detweilers' soup-
spoons, crosses D. and sets BOB'S *soupspoon, then*
exits to kitchen.)

FIONA. (*Rises, takes* FRANK'S *glass, crosses to* U. *doors*
and closes R. *door.*) Darling, I wish you'd look at that
drain, before it gets too late. And I've got to get ready.

FRANK. Yes, I'd better go get that coat hanger for the
drain. You haven't moved it, I hope.

FIONA. (*Crossing to kitchen.*) No, it's in back but I'd
go out the front door. It's knee-deep in the yard. (*Exits*
into kitchen with glasses.)

FRANK. Well, if you don't hear from me, call the Coast
Guard. (*Exits through* L. *double door, closing it as he*
goes.)

(BOB *picks up phone book, looks through it for the miss-*
ing Detweiler page, realizes it has been removed.
Puts down phone book, rises, sneaks up to door, tak-
ing cord jacket from coatrack, starts to put it on as
TERESA *enters.* TERESA *crosses to him.*)

TERESA. Where are you going?

BOB. Well, if I'm expected to spend an evening with
those two, I'm entitled to a drink.

TERESA. (*Picks up wine bottle.*) I've bought some.

BOB. (*Looking at the bottle.*) Oh, Jesus—

TERESA. (*Alarmed.*) The man in the liquor store
guaranteed it—

BOB. I'm going out. . . .

TERESA. You can't!

BOB. Watch me—

TERESA. For how long?

BOB. As long as it takes. . . . (*Goes out.*)

TERESA. (*Crosses to door with wine bottle.*) Bob . . .

BOB. (*Shouting back.*) It depends. . . . (TERESA
stands staring after him.)

TERESA. You can't just walk out. Bob . . . They'll be

here any minute. (*Crosses back to table, puts wine down, crosses to coatrack, takes plaid jacket, runs out after* BOB, *leaving door partially open.*) Bob!

(*The stage is empty for eight counts of silence, then* FOSTER *chimes ring, followed immediately by the* PHILLIPS *doorbell. A pause. They ring again. Pause. Finally* WILLIAM *and* MARY *enter, both in their 30s. He wears a soaking wet raincoat and hat and enters through* FOSTER *doors. She, although in a coat, is bone dry. She enters through* PHILLIPS *door and closes it.*)

WILLIAM. (*Calling.*) Hello. . . .

MARY. (*Calling.*) Hello. . . . (MARY *closes door. They look at each other, crossing* D. C. MARY *starts removing her gloves.*)

WILLIAM. Nobody here.

MARY. Funny.

WILLIAM. Strange.

MARY. (*Anxiously.*) We're not early, are we?

WILLIAM. No, of course not. (*Looks at his watch.*)

MARY. (*Calling off one way.*) Hello!

WILLIAM. Don't do that! Don't do that!

MARY. Just to let them know we're here.

WILLIAM. Well, we can wait quietly. Don't have to shout it around. They'll be here when they're ready, I suppose. . . .

MARY. Table's set.

WILLIAM. Oh, yes?

MARY. (*Nervously laughing.*) We're expected anyway. . . .

WILLIAM. (*Crosses* R.) Yes, well, of course.

MARY. (*Crosses* D. *to* WILLIAM.) Oh . . . I feel awful walking into their house like this . . .

WILLIAM. Now don't start to get nervous. There's nothing at all to get nervous about. Just stay calm. (MARY *has started to bite her nails.* WILLIAM *takes her hand from her mouth like he would a child's.*) Sit down if you like.

MARY. No, I won't sit down. . . . I . . .

WILLIAM. Did you take your pill?

MARY. Yes. . . .

WILLIAM. Good. Now you just have to be natural. You don't have to put on an act. There's no need.

MARY. It's just I can never think of anything to say.

WILLIAM. You don't have to if you don't want to. Nobody's asking you to say anything unless you feel you want to.

FIONA. (*Entering, crossing* U. C.) Darling, I . . . (*Crossing* D. *between* WILLIAM *and* MARY.) Oh, good heavens, you're here. Hello.

WILLIAM. Hello. Sorry to surprise you, but we rang a couple of times . . . didn't get an answer . . . the door was unlocked, so we . . .

FIONA. Oh, well, yes. That was very sensible of you. Frank must have left it open. He's cleaning out our drains. Heavens, you're soaked. Let me take your coat.

WILLIAM. Quite a downpour.

FIONA. Yes. What a downpour. (*Helps* WILLIAM *out of his coat and moves to his* R.) And how are you, Mary?

MARY. (*Inaudible.*) Fine. Thank you.

FIONA. Mmmm?

WILLIAM. Sinus. She's had a little sinus trouble, but it's much improved, isn't it, Mary?

FIONA. Oh, I'm sorry to hear that. I'll just put that in the hall, let it dry out. . . . Then we can all have a cocktail. . . . (FIONA *goes out* U.)

WILLIAM. Very charming, isn't she? Very charming woman.

MARY. (*In an undertone.*) I don't like cocktails.

WILLIAM. Well, just ask for a small glass, then.

MARY. But they give me terrible indigestion.

WILLIAM. Well, ask her for a stinger. You enjoyed the stinger you had at Bertha's at Christmas.

MARY. No, I didn't. Bertha just kept giving it to me. I didn't like it at all. Shall I ask her for a tonic?

WILLIAM. No, you can't ask her for a tonic. (*Crosses toward bar*, L.) People don't drink tonic. Not before dinner.

MARY. Well, what shall I say?

(FIONA *re-enters, closes door, crosses above table to bar.*)

FIONA. I've put it by the radiator. Should be dry in no time. Now what are we all going to have? Mary?

(WILLIAM *starts crossing* R. *above table, glaring and nodding at* MARY.)

MARY. Um . . .

FIONA. What would you like?

MARY. Er . . .

FIONA. Martini?

MARY. Well, I—

FIONA. Dry—or very, very dry?

MARY. (*At* WILLIAM's *nodded signals.*) Thank you very much.

FIONA. Good. (*Starts to make drinks.*) Very, very dry. William?

WILLIAM. (*Is right of* MARY.) Same again, please. (MARY *gives him a dirty look.*)

FIONA. Three very, very dry.

WILLIAM. Very nice room.

FIONA. Thank you.

WILLIAM. Very nice. Very tasteful.

FIONA. Frank is absolutely delighted you're joining the department. He speaks so highly of you. Awfully highly.

WILLIAM. Pleased to hear it. (MARY *smiles proudly at* WILLIAM.)

FIONA. Here we are, Mary. . . . (*Crosses with tray with three martinis, hands out the glasses, puts them on coffee table.*) Well, I suppose we drink to your new job, William.

WILLIAM. Well, thank you.

FIONA. Cheers, then.

WILLIAM. Bottoms up. (*They drink.* MARY *coughs.*)

FIONA. Oh, dear. Alright?

MARY. Thank you. Alright? (*Hiccups.*)

FIONA. You're absolutely miraculous with figures, apparently? (*Takes cigarettes from box on table with matches.*)

WILLIAM. Yes, well, I've always been interested in them. (*Takes matches from her.*) Seemed to come naturally. . . .

FIONA. In that case, I think you're so clever. I'm afraid I'm hopeless. I can't even add up the shopping list. (WILLIAM *finally gets the match to strike, after trying three or four times, and lights her cigarette.*) Then I'm afraid we women are all like that, aren't we?

WILLIAM. (*Prompting* MARY.) Yes.

MARY. Yes.

WILLIAM. I'm afraid you're right, there. I have to keep a firm eye on Mary's accounts, don't I, Mary?

MARY. Yes.

FIONA. Lucky you, Mary.

MARY. (*Smiles.*) Yes.

FIONA. Mary, please, sit down. (MARY *and* FIONA *sit on sofa, front* L.) Now what have you both been up to? Anything exciting?

WILLIAM. (*Standing* L. *of sofa.*) No, no.

FIONA. Oh. Well, it's been pretty dull all around for everyone, hasn't it? (*Pause.*) I mean, I think these things go in phases, don't they? (*Pause.*) You have an exciting time of the year. (*Puts ashes from cigarette in ashtray.*) And then all of a sudden you get a dull time of the year. (*Pause.*) I don't know why that should be, at all, do you? But I've always found that, for some reason. (*Crosses her legs. Pause.*) Must have something to do with the season of the year, I suppose.

WILLIAM. Ah!!!

FIONA. (*Takes a long drink,* WILLIAM *sips his.*) In the

summer you can always go out, can't you? But then you
get to winter, on a day like today, you can't do anything,
really, can you? (*Rises, crosses* U. C.) You're just stuck
indoors, all day, wishing you could get out only you can't.
Listen, I think I really ought to dash out and drag Frank
in. It's not fair for him to miss all the fun, is it? (*Goes
out* U.)

MARY. (*Puts glass down, rises, crosses,* R. *to above
sofa.*) She's very elegant, isn't she?

WILLIAM. (*Puts glass down on coffee table and crosses
to* MARY.) Oh, well. She's used to this sort of thing. Mr.
Foster must give dozens of this sort of informal dinner
parties. She's used to entertaining people. . . .

MARY. I don't think I could ever . . . (*Starts to nibble
her nails again.*)

WILLIAM. Oh, yes, you will. Yes, you will. You'll see.
We'll have to start doing this sort of thing soon, you
know.

MARY. Oh, I hope we don't . . .

WILLIAM. Well, people will expect it. You just can't
accept invitations and not return them. (*Slaps her again.*)
But don't worry. You'll find yourself enjoying this sort
of thing as much as she does. You'll see.

(PHILLIPS *DOORBELL rings.*)

MARY. (*Both look at door and turn back.*) What's
that?

WILLIAM. The bell.

(*The BELL rings.*)

MARY. Who is it?
WILLIAM. Somebody wanting to get in—
MARY. Who?

(*BELL rings.*)

WILLIAM. (*Crosses* R.) Go have a look.

MARY. Do you think I should?

(TERESA *appears in window of door.*)

WILLIAM. Go on. (MARY *goes. She admits* TERESA, *who is breathless.*)

TERESA. Hello—you're here.

WILLIAM. Hello, Terry.

MARY. Hello.

TERESA. This is very unusual . . . the guests letting the hostess in. (*Closes door.*)

WILLIAM. Very unusual.

MARY. That's alright.

WILLIAM. We rang the bell. (TERESA *crosses* L. *to kitchen door.*) Thought you must have all died. . . .

TERESA. No—actually—Bob's out . . . at the moment. He's just popped out . . . and I've been out as well, getting some air. . . . Forgot my key. Will you excuse me?—I just must check and see if Benjamin is alright.

MARY. How is he?

TERESA. Who?

MARY. Benjamin.

TERESA. Oh. Big, fat, and spoilt. No, actually he's terrific, but we don't tell him that or he'll get conceited, like his father. (*Exits.*)

WILLIAM. (*Looks at watch.*) Are you sure you got the telephone message right?

MARY. How do you mean?

WILLIAM. (*Crosses* D. *to* L. C.) She doesn't look exactly ready to entertain.

MARY. (*Crosses to* WILLIAM.) No. Friday night. I remember. She wanted us to come last night only we couldn't because we had to go to the Fosters'.

TERESA. (*Re-entering, with wet diaper, crosses above table to* L. *of* MARY.) Sorry. Take your coat, shall I? (*Gives wet diaper to* WILLIAM.)

MARY. Thank you. (*Removes her coat.* TERESA *takes coat, hangs it up, picks up clean diaper and baby talc from* U. *shelf.*)

WILLIAM. (*Notices that* MARY *is wearing her cardigan.*) Sweater!!!

MARY. What?

WILLIAM. (*Whispering loudly.*) Take off your sweater.

(MARY *takes off her cardigan and hides it under her right arm.*)

TERESA. (*Returning to* C.) My. That's lovely . . . it certainly is lovely. . . . (*Sees she's left* WILLIAM *holding diaper.*) Oh, I'm sorry. (*Takes diaper from* WILLIAM, *crosses below table and exits to kitchen.*)

WILLIAM. I think I'd better wash my hands. (*Takes the sweater from* MARY *and goes to hang it up. Wipes hand on his handkerchief, then sniffs at it.* MARY *crosses to* L. *of table.*)

TERESA. (*Re-entering to above table.*) Well, at least the weather's better than last night. Wasn't it terrible? (*Steps into kitchen area and gets tray, puts four blue wineglasses on it.*)

MARY. Yes, we were caught in it.

TERESA. (*Crosses to* R. *of table and wipes and sets down Mary's, hers and William's wineglasses.*) Were you . . . oh yes, how did that go?

WILLIAM. What's that?

TERESA. Your dinner with the big man. How did it go?

WILLIAM. Very pleasant. Very pleasant evening.

TERESA. Yes, isn't Frank the sweetest old thing?

MARY. Oh, yes, he's very, very nice. . . .

TERESA. And how was the fabulous Fiona?

WILLIAM. Charming. I found her very charming indeed.

TERESA. Yes, she's certainly that. What did you think, Mary? Have you met her before?

MARY. Only once. At the party. I thought she was quite—nice.

TERESA. (*Crosses down and sets Bob's wineglass.*) I just think she gets along better with the men. I'm sorry. I think she's a bitch.

WILLIAM. Oh, come now . . .

MARY. Could I have a peep at Benjamin?

TERESA. Certainly, but do you mind waiting until he's really asleep? Otherwise he'll be up all through dinner. I know him.

MARY. Alright.

TERESA. Please sit down. Make yourselves comfortable. I won't be a minute. (*Goes out.*)

WILLIAM. Sit, sit, sit. (MARY *crosses to desk. He crosses above sofa to desk; a pause.*) They could really make this room into something, if they put their minds to it.

MARY. I think Terry's looking awfully tired . . .

WILLIAM. Get it all repapered, touch of paint . . . make all the difference.

MARY. I wonder where Bob's gone?

WILLIAM. Gone out, didn't she say?

MARY. (*Sits, desk chair.*) That's what she said. I wonder why she invited us?

WILLIAM. For a meal.

MARY. She never has before. We hardly know her really. . . .

WILLIAM. I'm going to be working at the desk right next to him.

MARY. He didn't invite us. She did.

WILLIAM. I'm sure I don't know what you're going on about. (*Jiggling about.*)

MARY. What's the matter?

WILLIAM. Matter?

MARY. Why are you—?

WILLIAM. Nothing. Nothing at all. (*Paces a bit more.*) Just wondering where their—the whereabouts of their—that's all.

MARY. I don't know, I've not been here before. . . .

(FRANK *enters kitchen without shoes.* WILLIAM *and* MARY *are out of his line of sight.*)

FRANK. (*Singing as he enters from kitchen.*) Should

auld acquaintance be forgot . . . (*Crossing back to kitchen doorway.*) Darling, I thought you said Hansel and Gretel were here. . . .

WILLIAM. (*Picks up his drink from coffee table,* MARY *hers. Crosses to* D. C.) Oh, hello, Mr. Foster. (FRANK *crosses down, shakes his hand.*) Have you met my wife, Mary—Mr. Foster. (*Crosses to* R. *of* MARY.)

MARY. How do you do?

FRANK. Yes, of course we've met. One of those orgies. Christmas orgies at the office.

MARY. Imagine remembering . . .

FRANK. (*Crosses between* MARY *and* WILLIAM.) That's me, you see. Always remember the—good-looking women, never their ugly husbands. . . . (*Gives* WILLIAM *a dirty look.* WILLIAM *and* MARY *laugh politely.*) Matter of fact, let you in on a little secret. Everybody thinks that I promoted your husband because he's the best man at his job. But that's not the real reason. I'm after his lovely wife. Both drinking? Think I'll join you. Been out in the hurricane trying to open up a plugged drain. Pardon my socks. I put on some boots— (*Looks at* WILLIAM.) boots! —gave it a few jabs with the coat hanger, came back in, somebody stole my shoes . . .

WILLIAM. Stole them?

FRANK. Well, I wouldn't say stole them—moved them.

MARY. I'm always losing things.

FRANK. God love you.

WILLIAM. I'm always having to go round finding things for her.

FRANK. So's my wife. She's always complaining. Can I give you a refill?

WILLIAM. Thank you.

FRANK. Mary?

MARY. No, I think I've . . .

FRANK. Haven't put a dent in that yet? (*Crosses to bar.*) Want something else? Scotch? Bourbon? Manhattan?

MARY. No, thank you, I . . .

FRANK. What else have we got?

WILLIAM. (*Jigging up and down again.*) Excuse me—I wonder if I could just—

FRANK. Yes, yes, of course. Sit down. Make yourself at home. (WILLIAM *sits on* R. *of sofa.*) Now then. Let's see. Orange juice, ginger ale, soda, tonic . . .

MARY. Oh, well—!

FRANK. Tonic?

MARY. Yes.

FRANK. You got it. (*Opens a bottle of tonic and pours.*)

MARY. Thank you. (*Sits on* L. *of sofa, puts martini on coffee table.*)

WILLIAM. We were just saying, what a nice room this is.

FRANK. Room?

WILLIAM. Yes.

FRANK. (*Crosses above table with* MARY'S *tonic.*) Yes, I suppose it is. But then, I've seen it before, haven't I? Here we are. (*Picks up* MARY'S *martini, hands it to her, to her bewilderment.*) Cheers. (*He sips tonc—to his bewilderment.*)

WILLIAM. Cheers.

FRANK. Excuse me. (*Sits between them, puts his arms around them.*) You know, I'd like to say something to you both and—you can take it as you will. My wife and I . . . we've been married—well, it was our anniversary yesterday—for God knows how many years. And there are times when acrimony creeps in. In other words—we drive each other up the wall. And it is at times like these I say to myself, Frank, it's better than nothing. And the older you get, the better it is and the bigger the nothing. So my advice is, stick it out. Stick it out. Don't do things now that you're going to regret when you get too old like me to want to do them anymore. (*Pause.*) And that's all I have to say on the matter. Cheers. (*Toasts them.*)

WILLIAM and MARY. Cheers.

FIONA. (*Entering with* FRANK'S *shoes, crosses below to* L. *of sofa.*) Oh, hello— (WILLIAM *rises and steps to* R.

of sofa.) is Frank looking after you alright? Dinner won't be long.

FRANK. Oh good. I'm starved. I think we all are.

FIONA. Good. (*Crosses* C.) Frank, you left your shoes on top of the stove. I thought you might need them. (*Puts his shoes on the floor.*)

FRANK. (*Rises.*) Ah!

FIONA. What have you all been talking about, then? (*Crossing above sofa.*) Anything interesting?

FRANK. (*Significantly to* WILLIAM *and* MARY.) No, no, no . . . just chatting.

WILLIAM and MARY. Chatting.

FIONA. (*Loath to leave them.*) —Chatting?—Well . . . yes— Won't be too long now. (*Exits to kitchen.*)

FRANK. (*As he crosses to shoes, takes his dining-room chair, turns it around, facing* R., *sits and starts to put on shoes.*) Um. Thank you, dear.

WILLIAM. (*Hopping up and down a bit,* R. *of coffee table.*) Excuse me. Do you think I could just go up and wash my hands?

FRANK. Oh, yes, of course. I'd better give you the directions. Better explain the geography to you. (*Puts foot on coffee table to tie up the shoelace;* WILLIAM *moves the glasses to make room and* FRANK *misinterprets the gesture.*) Oh, thank you very much—just a loose bow, if you will. Well, you go up one flight, there's a door on your left. Pass that. Then you pass the door that's straight ahead of you as well. Now after that, if you sort of follow the hall which tends to double back on itself, if you see what I mean, the second door on your left, after you've turned that corner, is the guest room. Ready for the other one, are you? (*Puts the other foot on the table.*) If you want the bathroom, it's nearly diagonally opposite it, on your right.

WILLIAM. (*Crossing to* U. *door.*) Yes. Thank you.

FRANK. Oh! It's a little difficult to flush, by the way, but don't panic. You see we're away all summer and the hard water tends to lead to corrosion of that thing that's hooked to that wire that's attached to the plunger inside the tank where the water is.

WILLIAM. Right. (*Hurries out, closing doors.*)

FRANK. (*Puts chair back in place, turns and stares at* MARY, *who reacts nervously. He crosses, sits* L. *of her.*) My dear, a lot of men go through this sort of thing. But it blows over.

MARY. (*Looks to* U. *doors.*) It does?

FRANK. Invariably. Now, if you're in any sort of trouble at all . . . and you know the sort of trouble I mean . . . please feel that you can come and talk it over with me or my wife. (*Puts arm around* MARY.) I won't try and pretend that William isn't going to be a great asset to our department. And it's my job, insofar as it's possible, to see he's happy. (*Lifts* MARY's *chin.*) But that includes you, too, my dear.

MARY. Thank you.

FRANK. You see my wife filled me in about you.

MARY. Did she?

FRANK. Oh, yes. We don't have any secrets between us. She told me all about your little meeting . . .

MARY. What meeting?

FRANK. Last night.

MARY. I didn't go to any meeting—

FRANK. No, no, no. Your meeting with her. . . .

MARY. I was home last night. William was away, you see—

FRANK. Home?

MARY. Watching television.

FRANK. —I thought my wife said she— Television? Did you see that program about the three men . . .

MARY. Oh—yes, peculiar, wasn't it?

WILLIAM. (*Entering, crossing* D. C.) Found it on the first try.

FRANK. (*Rises, crosses to* WILLIAM.) Good for you.

WILLIAM. While I was in there, I took the liberty of easing the pin on your ball-cock.

FRANK. As long as you enjoyed yourself! (*Crosses*

above sofa.) Look, I'll just duck into the kitchen and see if the wife needs a hand. While I'm gone, you two feel perfectly free to talk. (WILLIAM *sits on* L. *of sofa.* FRANK *starts out, then turns.*) You know something? You're just a couple of silly kids. I've got a good notion to bang your heads together. (*Bangs their heads together and goes out to kitchen.*)

WILLIAM. Hasn't Mr. Foster got a great sense of humor?

MARY. (*Rises, crosses below coffee table to* U. C.) William . . .

WILLIAM. (*Rises.*) Yes?

MARY. He was just saying something very peculiar.

WILLIAM. (*Crosses to* MARY.) What sort of thing?

MARY. Well, I don't know, but he seemed to be saying . . .

WILLIAM. What?

MARY. No, it's silly. (*Nibbles her nails.* WILLIAM *corrects her again.*)

WILLIAM. I'm afraid you're being more incoherent than usual tonight, Mary. I'm not following you at all.

(*DOOR SLAMS and* TERESA *enters with tray, four cups, four saucers and a corkscrew on it, and goes to the* R. *of table.*)

TERESA. I've been . . . trying to get everything ready. I don't know what's happened to Bob, I'm sure.

MARY. (*Crosses to* L. *of table.*) Can we help?

TERESA. No, thank you, I think I've done most of it now. (*Picks up wine bottle and corkscrew.*) Oh, I tell you what. If you're feeling strong, William, I wonder if you'd . . .

WILLIAM. Yes, of course. (*Takes bottle and corkscrew and proceeds to open it.*)

MARY. Have you gotten Benjamin off to sleep?

TERESA. (*Crosses* D. *and puts Bob's soup cup and saucer down at his place.*) Oh yes, he's alright. Not a sound out of him. You wanted to take a peek, didn't you?

MARY. Oh, could I? I'll be very quiet.

TERESA. (*Crosses* U. *to kitchen door.*) It's alright. Once he's off, he's off. Through the kitchen and—oh, you'll find it.

MARY. (*Going.*) Thank you. (*Goes off.* TERESA *stares after her, crosses to table, sets down hers and Detweilers' cups and saucers.*)

TERESA. (*To* WILLIAM.) Can you manage?

WILLIAM. (*Crosses to* D. C.) Oh yes. Yes, I've opened one or two in my time, I can tell you. (*Strains, trying to get cork out of bottle.*)

TERESA. Yes, I can imagine. (*Pause.*) That's where Bob is.

WILLIAM. Where?

TERESA. In a bar.

WILLIAM. I've heard he enjoys a drink. He's usually in the bar with that crowd from the office at lunchtime. I've seen them all going in there.

TERESA. You don't drink at lunch, then?

WILLIAM. (*Still struggling with cork.*) Oh, no. I'd be fast asleep. No, as a matter of fact, I drink very sparingly, altogether.

TERESA. How did you survive with Bob the other night, then?

WILLIAM. Other night?

TERESA. On that binge you both had.

WILLIAM. Binge? When was this?

TERESA. Couple of nights ago. When was it? Wednesday.

WILLIAM. Not Wednesday. I was in Baltimore on Wednesday.

TERESA. Baltimore?

WILLIAM. (*Crosses up to her.*) Yes. First Wednesday of every month. I spend the night—visit our branch there.

(*Cork suddenly pops from bottle.*)

TERESA. Baltimore?

WILLIAM. Anything wrong?

TERESA. Have you ever been out for a drink with Bob?

WILLIAM. No. I said I wasn't the drinking . . .

TERESA. Have you ever . . . discussed your marriage with Bob at all?

WILLIAM. Discussed it, how do you mean?

TERESA. (*Suddenly angry.*) Talked to him about it, in detail. I think that you know what I mean, William.

WILLIAM. Certainly not, no. I don't believe in—

TERESA. (*Crosses D. with tray.*) Thank you. That's all I want to know. Thank you very much. (*Puts Bob's dishes and silverware on tray, crosses to front door and throws tray and dishes out. Crosses to above table, picks up glass, holds it out for* WILLIAM *to pour drink, which he does.*) Well—that's it. As far as I'm concerned, that's it. (*Drinks.*)

WILLIAM. What's it?

TERESA. *That*—is—it. Up his! (*Takes another drink.*)

WILLIAM. Easy now.

TERESA. I'm going to get the dinner. I'm going to be absolutely, madly, permissively modern. (*Moves in to him.*) I am going to serve up the food and then, in the absence of our lord and master, who is probably groveling on the floor with some topless hostess by now, we will all sit down, have a marvelous gourmet dinner. (*Crosses to kitchen.*)

MARY. (*Entering, crosses between* WILLIAM *and* TERESA.) Isn't he beautiful?

TERESA. (*Hostilely.*) Who's beautiful?

MARY. (*Turning to* TERESA.) Benjamin. He's the spitting image of Bob, isn't he? Just like his daddy.

TERESA. Oh, yes. You mean the same squat, piggy little face.

MARY. Oh, no, I didn't . . .

TERESA. Same nature, too. Screams for what he wants till he gets it. He'll be a real charmer when he grows up. Just like his father . . . that sonofabitch! (TERESA *goes out.*)

(MARY *and* WILLIAM *in stunned silence, then:*)

MARY. What's wrong?
WILLIAM. Something very wrong, I'm afraid.
MARY. What?
WILLIAM. I don't know. Something to do with Baltimore.
MARY. Baltimore?
WILLIAM. And Bob's drinking. Then she took his dishes and threw them out the door.
MARY. Maybe the dinner's burned.
WILLIAM. No. It's more serious than that.
MARY. Oh.

(FIONA *enters, crosses* D. *of table with tray with four dishes of avocado, puts tray in serving cart.*)

FIONA. At last. You must have thought we'd all gone to bed or something. Now, Mary, I've put you there. And William there. (WILLIAM *croses to chair* L. *of table.*) Do sit down. Frank's just digging us up something to drink. (MARY *sits.* WILLIAM *starts to sit, then waits for* FIONA. WILLIAM *and* MARY *are on swivel chairs which can swing through ninety degrees to take in* BOB *and* TERESA'S *section as well.*) Now, I hope you like avocado. I know some people loathe them. (*Serving dishes to all four places.*) Now this is all going to be terribly informal, so please don't expect anything elaborate. If I've forgotten to give you anything, don't hesitate to ask. At the rate Frank's going he'll probably join us for coffee, but please do start.

(TERESA *slams kitchen door.* WILLIAM *and* MARY *swivel.* TERESA *enters with tureen of soup, puts it on the table.*)

MARY. Can we help, Terry?
TERESA. No, it's alright. I can manage perfectly, thank you. (*Sits.*) I have everything under control, I think. Just

help yourselves—please help yourselves— Can you smell it?

WILLIAM. What?

TERESA. (*Rushing out.*) Burning! Burning.

MARY. (*Starting to ladle the soup into cups.*) Soup, William? (*Loud crashing of pots and pans offstage.*) Soup, William?

WILLIAM. Thank you.

(MARY *serves* WILLIAM'S *soup. He starts to taste it, smells spoon, sniffs cup, then smells spoon again.*)

MARY. What are you doing?

WILLIAM. It smells of air-freshener.

MARY. No.

WILLIAM. Definitely air-freshener.

MARY. Well, try and eat it. She's gone to a lot of trouble.

WILLIAM. You know what happens to my stomach with badly cooked food—

MARY. Yes, dear, I know.

(WILLIAM *and* MARY *swivel.* FRANK *enters with an opened bottle of white wine.*)

FRANK. Whoever put this cork in did a good job. Been dancing round the kitchen trying to get it out.

FIONA. Sit down, darling.

FRANK. Right. (*Sits, puts wine on table.*) Ah. Now then. What have we got here?

FIONA. Avocado, you've had it before.

FRANK. Yes, I know I've had it before. Didn't recognize it, that's all.

(FRANK *pours* MARY'S *wine.* TERESA *slams kitchen door.* WILLIAM *and* MARY *swivel.* TERESA *enters.*)

TERESA. That stove! That damn stove. I have asked

Bob a hundred times— Well, I'm not waiting for him.
He can damn well starve to death!

MARY. Terry, is anything the matter?

(FRANK *has finished pouring* MARY's *and his wine, rises,
crosses to* FIONA *and pours hers.*)

TERESA. Matter? Matter? Good heavens, no. Come on
then. Let's enjoy yourselves—eat up—

MARY. Right. This looks delicious. (*Picks up her spoon.*
WILLIAM *continues to gaze at his plate, dubiously.*)

TERESA. William?

WILLIAM. Er, yes, thank you. . . . (WILLIAM *and*
MARY *swivel.* TERESA *crosses to kitchen area and gets
croutons.*)

FRANK. (*Pouring* WILLIAM's *wine.*) William?

WILLIAM. Yes, thank you. (WILLIAM *and* MARY *swivel.*
TERESA *crosses to table with croutons, puts some in each
cup and in tureen. Having filled* WILLIAM's *wineglass,*
FRANK *crosses back and sits in his chair.*)

TERESA. I hope you enjoy this soup. I stood over it for
hours. (WILLIAM *and* MARY *dip their spoons in the soup.*)
I've put practically everything into it I could lay my
hands on. . . . (WILLIAM *and* MARY *each take a mouth-
ful.*) Benjamin helped me with it a little bit. (WILLIAM
and MARY *choke.*)

MARY. (*Recovering.*) Aren't you having any?

TERESA. I couldn't face it just at the moment. Don't
mind me. I'll just get drunk. . . .

(WILLIAM *and* MARY *swivel.* TERESA *pours glass of wine,
takes wine, crosses up to front door, opens it and
looks out.*)

FRANK. This doesn't taste like avocado at all to me.
Tastes like canned pineapple.

FIONA. Darling, if you're going to complain, the best
thing to do is not to eat it.

FRANK. I'm not complaining. I like canned pineapple better.

(WILLIAM *and* MARY *swivel.*)

TERESA. (*Crossing back to table.*) How is it?
MARY. Wonderful.   WILLIAM. Very unusual.
TERESA. (*Picking up ladle.*) I can't resist it. I'm going to have to give it a try. (*Sips soup.*) It tastes like anti-perspirant. Doesn't it taste like anti-perspirant to you—it must—
MARY. No, it doesn't.
WILLIAM. Yes, it does!
TERESA. Then what the hell are you eating it for, for God's sake? Here, let me pour it back. (*Gets the cups and pours the soup back into the tureen.*) Well, that's that— End of the meal.
WILLIAM. Ah.
TERESA. (*Cheerfully.*) Never mind. There's always the wine, isn't there? (*Pours glass of wine.*) The least we can do is behave like civilized human beings. I don't know about you two but I'm going to enjoy myself. (*Starts to sing:*) "I've been working on the railroad, all the livelong day, I've been working on the railroad, just to pass the time away."

(WILLIAM *and* MARY *swivel.*)

FRANK. What's next, dear?
FIONA. Oh, just a little Danish dish.
FRANK. Is she pretty? (WILLIAM *laughs.*)
FIONA. No, dear, it's veal and pork.
FRANK. Oh, well, I suppose we'll recognize her when we see her. Speaking of recognizing things, we had a little fellow in the office once. Came from somewhere down south. Perkins, was it? No, it was Porter—Porterhouse. Some name like that.
FIONA. Darling, do eat.

FRANK. No, it was Carter. That's it. Billy Carter. Anyway, he came from down south. He had the most terrible wife. Now, it was just before the office Christmas party and the boss decided to put Mrs. Carter in charge of the —that was not her name. What was her name now?

FIONA. Darling, we are all simply panting for our second course.

(WILLIAM *and* MARY *swivel.*)

TERESA. (*Singing:*) "Dinah, won't you blow, Dinah, won't you blow, Dinah, won't you blow your horn?" (*Turns to* WILLIAM.) Thank you, Mary.—William, did you ever hear that very funny joke about the wife who came home unexpectedly and found her husband in bed with the baby sitter. . . .

WILLIAM. No. I don't believe we ever did. . . .

TERESA. Well. There they both were, you see. Him and this girl . . .

WILLIAM. Terry, I wonder if I could just . . .

TERESA. They're humping away on the bed, you see . . . and the wife just stands there and says . . .

(PHILLIPS *DOORBELL rings.*)

WILLIAM. Isn't that the bell?

TERESA. The wife says—let it ring—she says to her husband very sweetly . . .

(*The DOORBELL rings again.*)

WILLIAM. I think that's the bell.

TERESA. (*Sharply.*) Let it ring. She says to him, terribly sweetly, "Darling, you can practice till you're blue in the face, but you'll never get it right."

MARY. (*Laughs nervously.*) William, what's humping?

WILLIAM. (*Sharply.*) Mary!

(MARY *stops laughing.* WILLIAM *and* MARY *swivel.*)

FRANK. (*Suddenly remembering.*) Fraser! That was her name. Mrs. Fraser. That was it.

FIONA. (*Rising to clear table.*) Well done, dear. I'll just get the rest. (MARY *rises to help.*) Now sit still, Mary. I can manage. (MARY *passes dirty plates.*)

FRANK. Anyway, Mrs.—I forgot what I was telling you—

WILLIAM. The boss was organizing this office Christmas party—

FRANK. Right. And Mrs. er—

MARY. Mrs. Carter—

FRANK. Carter? That wasn't her name—

WILLIAM. Mrs. Fraser—

FRANK. That's it, Mrs.— Wait a minute. I have a feeling her name wasn't Fraser, either. I was thinking of somebody else.

FIONA. (*As she crosses to kitchen with the dirty plates.*) Darling, you really are becoming awfully tedious. . . . (*Goes out.*)

(*The DOORBELL RINGS.* WILLIAM *and* MARY *swivel.*)

WILLIAM. (*Rising.*) I think I'd better answer it.

TERESA. It's entirely up to you, Bill. I'm not answering anything. I'm going to enjoy my dinner.

WILLIAM. (*Looks out window of the door.*) It's Bob. (*Opens door.*) He looks a little . . .

(BOB *enters with a beer can in hand.*)

BOB. (*Singing:*)
        "Hail, hail, the gang's all here.
            What the hell do we care,
            What the hell do we care?"
(*Speaking.*) All feeding our faces, are we? Filling ourselves with goodies? Lucky you. Did you cook anything for me, my love, or do I go out to a hamburger joint?

TERESA. Oh God!

BOB. (*Sings "Ta-Ra-Ra-Boom-De-Ay," producing a beer can from each inside and outside coat pocket, places them on table.*) There's Mary the Mouse. Hello, Mary the Mouse, how are you?

MARY. Hello—Bob—

BOB. (*Crossing to* WILLIAM.) Well, then, how have things been going? (*Kisses* WILLIAM *several times.*) Sit down, William, don't mind me. . . . (*As* WILLIAM *crosses* BOB, BOB *gooses him.* WILLIAM *sits at table very embarrassed.* BOB *closes door.* BOB *leans against wall.*) All been telling each other dirty stories?

TERESA. Yes. I've heard some very dirty stories, thank you.

BOB. I thought you might. I thought you'd root that out sooner or later.

TERESA. Well, I did. . . .

BOB. Good.

(WILLIAM *and* MARY *swivel.*)

FIONA. (*Entering with two vegetable dishes, crosses below table to serving cart.*) More to come.

(*During the following dialogue,* BOB *turns to coatrack, takes off coat and shirt together, takes shirt out of coat, ties shirt around waist like an apron, takes handkerchief out of his pocket and lays it over his arm.*)

WILLIAM. Are you sure you can manage?

FIONA. Yes, thank you, William. Frank will give me a hand. Won't you, darling? (*Crosses to* R. *of table.*)

FRANK. What? Oh yes. You should have told me. (*Rises and follows* FIONA.)

FIONA. (*Crossing to kitchen.*) It's fairly obvious, darling. I don't have to tell you, surely. You can see me, staggering in and out, laden with dishes.

(FIONA *and* FRANK *go out.* BOB *turns to table as* WILLIAM *and* MARY *swivel.*)

BOB. All right, who's for a beer then? Eh? Mary?

MARY. No, thank you.

BOB. William, I know you'll have one.

WILLIAM. —Er, no, thanks, Bob. Got the wine, thank you.

BOB. (*Aggressive.*) Come on. Have a beer.

TERESA. Bob, we're having dinner. (*Rises.*) Either sit down or shut up.

BOB. Why should I shut up? I'm just offering our friends a drink, that's all.

TERESA. (*Dangerously quiet.*) I'm warning you, I'll throw something.

BOB. Oh, good. They'll enjoy that.. (*Crosses* D. R. *of table to his place.*) She's got a good arm. Hit a wall once with a plate of spaghetti at twenty paces. You don't believe me? I've seen her do it. . . . Right, four beers it is, then. (*Sits.*)

(TERESA *sits.* WILLIAM *and* MARY *swivel.*)

FIONA. (*Entering, crosses above table, puts dish on table.*) Do stop fussing, darling. They're not as hot as all that. I think this has turned out alright. I hope so.

FRANK. (*Following her on, crosses* D. *of table, puts plates at her place on table.*) Smells a bit off to me. (*Crosses and sits in his chair.*)

FIONA. (*Sighing.*) Darling. (*Places the dishes and starts to serve onto plates.*)

(WILLIAM *and* MARY *swivel.*)

BOB. Here we are, Mary. One for you.

MARY. No, really, Bob, I . . .

TERESA. Bob, she doesn't want any. . . .

BOB. Well, she's having it whether she likes it or not. I can't sit here drinking alone. It's goddamn unsociable. . . .

WILLIAM. Now listen, Bob, I don't think you should—

BOB. Oh, shut up—

TERESA. You really are a son-of-a-bitch, aren't you? A rude drunken son-of-a-bitch.

MARY. I really think we ought to go. . . .

WILLIAM. Yes, I think . . .

TERESA. (*Rises.*) Don't go. If anyone's going, it's the son-of-a-bitch.

BOB. Me?

TERESA. Yes, you.

(WILLIAM *and* MARY *swivel.* BOB *rises, crosses* U. L.)

FIONA. (*Passing plates.*) William, you know it's terrible having a husband with absolutely no palate.

WILLIAM. Oh, dear. I'm so sorry.

(WILLIAM *and* MARY *swivel.*)

BOB. If I want to stay here, I'll stay here. (*Moves closer to* TERESA, *half menacing.*)

(WILLIAM *and* MARY *swivel.*)

FIONA. That's why Frank doesn't really enjoy these occasions.

FRANK. Oh, yes I do. I'm enjoying it very much.

MARY. Oh, yes. So am I.

(WILLIAM *and* MARY *swivel.*)

TERESA. I'm warning you, Bob. (*Picks up ladle.*)

WILLIAM. Terry, I don't think I should . . .

TERESA. Bob.

BOB. Go on then, I dare you—

(*They approach each other.* WILLIAM *and* MARY *swivel.*)

FRANK. Hey! You interrupted my story about Mrs. Whatshername. Now then . . . (*Pauses for thought.*

TERESA *swings at* BOB *with soup ladle. He ducks it and catches her wrist.* WILLIAM *and* MARY *swivel.* TERESA *and* BOB *struggle silently.*) She was put in charge of refreshments for the office Christmas party—and what do you think she served us? Take a guess. (WILLIAM *and* MARY *swivel.* TERESA *drops ladle, kicks* BOB. *He yells.* WILLIAM *and* MARY *swivel.* TERESA *runs* D. R. C. BOB *follows and catches her.*) Give up? Linguine with clam sauce. What do you think of that? (WILLIAM *and* MARY *swivel.* TERESA *bites* BOB. *He yells.* WILLIAM *and* MARY *swivel.* TERESA *runs* D. *of table* L., BOB *runs* U. *of table* L., *stops her before she can get to the kitchen door. She turns, runs* D. *of table and he follows, and they both exit to kitchen.*) Christmas office party, everybody falling down drunk, holding plates of linguine and clam sauce.

(WILLIAM *and* MARY *swivel.*)

MARY. (*Rises.*) Is anything the matter?
WILLIAM. Bob, I don't think this is really . . .

(WILLIAM *and* MARY *swivel.*)

FRANK. Chairman of the Board got it all over his shoes—

(WILLIAM *and* MARY *swivel.* TERESA *screams offstage.*)

BOB. (*Offstage.*) Bitch!

(WILLIAM *and* MARY *swivel.*)

FRANK. He turns on this woman—Mrs. Taylor—that's it—and he says, now let me get this right, he says—

(*DOOR SLAMS.* WILLIAM *and* MARY *swivel.*)

TERESA. Goddamn you.

(WILLIAM *and* MARY *swivel.*)

FRANK. Well, he really let her have it. And Mrs. Taylor, who's blind herself by then says—how did she put it now . . .

(WILLIAM *and* MARY *swivel.*)

TERESA. (*Enters, backing* R. *of table.*) Keep away, Bob —keep away. I'm warning you. (*Picks up soup tureen.*)
WILLIAM. Bob, for God's sake . . .

(WILLIAM *and* MARY *swivel.*)

FRANK. I know what she said.

(WILLIAM *and* MARY *swivel.* TERESA *draws back with soup tureen.*)

WILLIAM. Terry!
MARY. No!

(WILLIAM *leaps up between* TERESA *and* BOB. TERESA *throws the soup—it hits* WILLIAM *square on.* WILLIAM *sits.* WILLIAM *and* MARY *swivel.*)

FRANK. That's right! Mrs. Taylor says . . . (TERESA *runs out the front door.* BOB *follows her.*) Mrs. Taylor says . . . you're wet!
WILLIAM. (*Laughing.*) Oh! Very good!
FRANK. No, no. You are wet.
WILLIAM. (*Rises.*) Oh! Oh dear, there must be a drip. (*They all look up at the ceiling.*)
FRANK. (*Rises.*) Drip?

(FIONA *rises, as does* MARY.)

FIONA. Darling, you haven't left the shower on again?
FRANK. Of course not. Anyway, he isn't standing under the shower. He's under the—er—other place. (*They all gaze toward the ceiling.*)

CURTAIN

ACT TWO

SCENE 1

*The same. Saturday morning. A sign hangs on the inside
of* TERESA'S *front door, saying "Good-bye Forever."
The Portapram is gone.*

BOB. (*Entering with Bromo in glass.*) Terry! Terry!
(*Stares around, sees sign, toasts sign, then sits in chair.*
FRANK *enters in his running sweatsuit, jogging. Crosses
to* L. *of coffee table. He jogs up and down, looking at the
timer on table, waiting for it to ring. It doesn't. Finally
he loses patience, picks it up and shakes it. Apparently
it's broken.* FRANK *glares at it and marches off with it to
the kitchen.* PHILLIPS *DOORBELL RINGS.* BOB *rises.*)
Home again, eh? (*Crosses to door, opens it, turns and
crosses to kitchen doorway. He does not see that it is*
MARY *standing outside.*) Wouldn't kindly old mother
shelter little red riding drawers from the big bad wolf—

(*It is* MARY *with a load of homemade pound cake in
baking pan with a ribbon.*)

MARY. Hello.
BOB. Come in. Do come in.
MARY. (*Shuts door behind her.*) Thank you. (*Peers
around.*)
BOB. (*Crossing to* MARY.) A little chillier this morning,
don't you think? Though it might warm up later. Don't
like the look of those clouds, though, do you? Could have
a little rain, don't you agree? Or even snow. You know
what they say—red sky in the morning, shepherd's warning. Red sky at night, your roof is alight. What can I do
for you?

MARY. I—

BOB. (*Courteously.*) Sit down.

MARY. (*Awkwardly doing so in armchair.*) Thank you.

BOB. Can I—do anything for you?

MARY. No. I just wanted a word with Terry.

BOB. She's not here.

MARY. Will she be back?

BOB. That's not likely.

MARY. Oh, I see.

BOB. All the signs seem to indicate she's gone for good.

MARY. Oh.

BOB. She's walked out before, you see, but I've been making a quick inventory and this time she seems to have taken quite a comprehensive collection of essential items with her. One nightie, one toothbrush, at least two sets of underwear, a long-playing record of Aaron Copland's "Fanfare for a Common Man" and—the baby. (*Crosses to rocker.*)

MARY. What made her go?

BOB. I don't know. She may have eloped with the editor of the *Village Voice*.

MARY. Oh, who's he?

BOB. Yes.—Well— (*Sits in rocker.*) Failing that, I repeat, what can I do for you?

MARY. Well—if we could help in any way?

BOB. Help?

MARY. After last night . . . That soup and things . . . I just thought that if there was anything that William and I could do to help?

BOB. No, that's all cleaned up, thank you.

MARY. I didn't mean that.

BOB. You didn't?

MARY. I meant—help—you know.

BOB. That's very nice of you.

MARY. (*Warming.*) I mean, I thought that if you and William were going to be working together, we ought . . .

BOB. We ought to be able to get together. Right?

MARY. Right! William always says—

BOB. Where is he?

MARY. Excuse me?

BOB. William, where is he?

MARY. Oh.

BOB. He knows you're here, doesn't he?

MARY. Well.

BOB. He doesn't?

MARY. No—this was my idea. William always says that I'm too . . . retiring. That I must get interested, talk to people. Because it's important to talk to people, isn't it? Making social contact is essential. If you're going to have people come over and drink martinis and things, you must be able to converse with them. So I thought, well, perhaps the first thing to do is to get to know Terry and you. Perhaps talk over problems. That sort of thing— just generally sort of help. (*Crosses to him.*) I mean, that's what we're on this earth for, isn't it?

BOB. Good point.

MARY. (*Hands him cake, crosses back and sits in chair.*) Thank you.

BOB. No, thank you. Yes. You're right. Well, there's a broom in the kitchen closet and I think you'll find the mop right next to it.

MARY. What . . . ?

BOB. No, I'll tell you what. Let's not take advantage of friendship. Two bucks an hour, how's that? Three bucks when you're using the vacuum cleaner because that's pretty heavy.

MARY. I may come back. (*Starting to get up.*)

BOB. Sit down.

MARY. No, I really must be . . .

BOB. Sit down.

MARY. Don't you think you can talk to me the way you talk to Terry.

BOB. I wouldn't dream of it. (*Rises, crosses* U.) Look, I'd hate you to go away feeling that I'm ungrateful. I'm not. (*Hands her empty pan after turning it upside down and removing cake.*) Come on, buck up. I'll go put on a shirt, you go and make us some coffee and then we'll both sit down here and I'll tell you all about my marriage. How would you like that?

MARY. No. . . .

BOB. No pleasing you, is there? All right, you tell me about your problems.

MARY. I don't have any problems.

BOB. That's O.K., we'll invent some. This could be fun. (*Crosses to kitchen and gets apron from cabinet.*)

MARY. I ought to go.

(FRANK *enters with the broken timer and a screwdriver, and a cup of coffee; sits, sofa—puts coffee on table and starts to fiddle with the works of the timer.*)

BOB. (*Crosses in, throws apron to* MARY.) Make the coffee. . . . You may even find a cup on the drainboard if you dig deep enough. (*Goes out.*)

MARY. (*Rises, crosses to kitchen.*) Bob . . . Bob . . . (*Turns, crosses to chair, picks up purse, puts pan into it, sits, looking toward kitchen.*)

(FRANK *drops a bit of the timer into his coffee and attempts to fish it out with the screwdriver. The* FOSTER *DOOR CHIME rings.* FRANK *goes out to answer it.* MARY *rises, crosses to coatrack, hangs apron, turns, and as she does,* BOB *enters and sees her, pulls his belt off, which startles* MARY, *then holds belt in his hand and snaps it, and* MARY *takes the apron and runs into the kitchen, followed by an amused* BOB. FRANK *enters, followed by* TERESA, *who is pulling front end of a baby carriage into view through* FOSTER *main doors.*)

FRANK. Well, this is very unexpected, Terry.

TERESA. Yes. I know that. I'm sorry.

FRANK. No, no—a pleasure. A pleasure. Baby'll be alright in his—what do you call that thing?

TERESA. Portapram.

FRANK. Portapram! He looks sweet snug all tucked in.
(*Leans over the Portapram.*) Oh-hoo.

TERESA. Oh, please—don't do that. Let him sleep.
(*Closes* L. FOSTER *door.* FRANK *closes* R. FOSTER *door.*)
It must have been the bus ride. As soon as we got on he
dropped off.

FRANK. Dropped off?

TERESA. To sleep.

FRANK. Oh. Please sit down.

TERESA. (*Crosses, sits on* R. *end of sofa.* FRANK *follows,
stands* L. *of sofa.*) Thanks.

FRANK. Can I get you some coffee?

TERESA. No, thank you.

FRANK. I'd give you mine but there's some machinery
in it. Now, what can I do for you?

TERESA. I was on the bus, you see . . .

FRANK. Were you? Yes. Nothing like a bus ride on a
Saturday morning.

TERESA. I was on my way to my mother's . . .

FRANK. Ah! Were you? Wonderful the way you young
people communicate with your parents.

TERESA. And I thought I must talk to someone. *Anyone.*
Then the bus passed your street and I thought of you. So
I got off.

FRANK. Glad you did. Glad you did. Although your
mother will be disappointed. What'd you do with old Bob,
send him on ahead?

TERESA. I've left him, Frank.

FRANK. Where?

TERESA. We've separated. At least I have.

FRANK. (*Crosses* D. L. C., *stunned.*) You're kidding,
you're pulling my leg. This is shocking news, Terry. Absolutely shocking. I don't know what to say— I— For
heaven's sake.

TERESA. I don't know who this other woman is, but . . .

FRANK. Woman?

TERESA. He's got another woman.

FRANK. *Another* another woman? You have no idea who she is, I guess? (*Crosses* U. *between chairs to* L. *of sofa.*)

TERESA. No idea.

FRANK. Fiona'll be shattered, you know.

TERESA. Will she?

FRANK. Absolutely. She's terribly fond of both of you.

TERESA. So I'm being boringly conventional and running home to Mother.

FRANK. (*Sits on sofa.*) You'll be alright with her, won't you?

TERESA. I doubt it. We'll be at each other's throats in five minutes. I think she really prefers Bob. I'm too much like my father.

FRANK. Well, I'd talk to him, then.

TERESA. No, he left us in 1953.

FRANK. Listen, Terry, are you absolutely certain about this?

TERESA. Yes. He left us eighteen years ago.

FRANK. No, I mean—you and Bob. You're such a cute little couple—cute little apartment—cute little baby. Your whole future in front of you. Oh, I know we all make jokes about Bob being the office Romeo . . .

TERESA. Really? I didn't know that.

FRANK. No, no, no. Men's jokes. Nothing serious.

TERESA. This is serious.

FRANK. Yes, of course. Are you really sure of your facts? Do you have any concrete evidence?

TERESA. Yes. Yes. Staying out till all hours of the morning . . .

FRANK. Yes, well, that isn't really evidence. I mean, take me for instance. I could say—where on earth is Fiona at the moment. And the answer would be—I haven't the slightest idea. But I certainly don't imagine she's in bed with the fellow next door. She's probably at the hairdresser's.

TERESA. She doesn't stay at the hairdresser's till three o'clock in the morning, does she?

FRANK. No, I don't think she does.

TERESA. Well, then.

FRANK. She has been out that late, though.

TERESA. Has she?

FRANK. (*Rises, crosses to* U. C.) Not often, but occasionally. Why, only the other day—when was it—last wedding anniversary—Wednesday, she was out till all hours.

TERESA. Wednesday?

FRANK. Yes, Wednesday. Really very late.

TERESA. Wednesday?

FRANK. (*Crosses to* L. *of sofa.*) But you don't want to talk about me—it's your problems we're concerned with.

TERESA. Wednesday.

FRANK. Tell you what I'll do. I'll have a word with Bob—see if I can get to the bottom of it. He'll have to listen to me.

TERESA. (*Suddenly getting it.*) Yes!

FRANK. (*Picking up phone to dial.*) Yes! I'll read him the riot act.

TERESA. Oh! No.

FRANK. No? Oh, well. (*Replaces the phone.*) Second thoughts are often best. Look, are you sure I can't get you something to drink?

TERESA. (*Thoughtfully.*) No, thank you.

FRANK. Tea? Coffee? It's all ready, I just made some.

TERESA. Thank you.

FRANK. You will?

TERESA. Yes, please. Oh, yes.

FRANK. (*Crossing* U.) Yes! (*Turns back.*) Black or cream?

TERESA. Black, please.

FRANK. (*Starts to kitchen.*) Right. (*Turns back.*) Coffee.

TERESA. Yes, please.

FRANK. Right. (*Goes out to kitchen.*)

(MARY *enters wearing apron and crosses to rocker and*

dusts, then crosses to phone table and dusts, crosses to bookshelf U. and dusts and picks up clippings. BOB enters, still just in slacks with towel around his neck, crosses to MARY.)

BOB. What are you doing?
MARY. *(Startled.)* Oh. Just tidying up.
BOB. Where's my coffee?
MARY. *(Crosses to desk, dusting.)* You won't get any if you talk like that.
BOB. *(Crosses D. C.)* Look, would you mind leaving my house alone?
MARY. I'm only cleaning up a little.
BOB. Well, don't. My wife spent a great deal of time and trouble accumulating that dust. And in five minutes you've undone years of her work.
MARY. Don't be silly.
BOB. You're a home wrecker. That's what you are . . .
MARY. *(Taking piles of papers from desk.)* You don't want a dirty house, do you?
BOB. Why not?
MARY. Well . . . it's dirty.
BOB. Look. Do me a favor and make the goddamn coffee.
MARY. *(Crosses D. to kitchen.)* You are very, very, very rude. I don't know how Terry puts up with you. . . . *(Turns to BOB, who throws towel over his head and growls loudly and waves his arms. She gasps and runs off, followed by BOB.)*

(FIONA enters with dress box, crosses between PHILLIPS chair and sofa.)

FIONA. Hello, Terry. How are you?
TERESA. Oh, quite well. . . .
FIONA. I wondered what that squirming lump was in the hall. It's your baby, isn't it?
TERESA. Probably.

FIONA. Sweet. That's an adorable stroller.

TERESA. It's actually a Portapram.

FIONA. (*Crosses above* PHILLIPS *chair.*) Oh, is that what it is? It's lovely. Sweetie, you won't mind my saying so, but it looks as if he's drooled just a teeny bit on the carpet.

TERESA. Oh dear.

FIONA. It doesn't matter as long as he's all right. (*Crosses to* FOSTER *chair, puts package and bag in chair, starts to remove gloves.*) It's a dull carpet anyway, probably brighten it up.

FRANK. (*Enters with a cup, crosses to* FIONA.) Ah, Fiona. Thank God you're here. Get ready to brace yourself.

FIONA. Why?

FRANK. Terry's just dropped a bombshell.

FIONA. Has she?

FRANK. Bob's got another woman—

FIONA. (*Sits on dress box.*) Another one? (*When she recovers her composure she removes dress box from under her.*)

FRANK. A lover, dear. A love affair.

FIONA. Oh. Well—I'm—absolutely amazed.

FRANK. They've split up.

FIONA. Really?

FRANK. (*Crosses* D. L. C.) Terry's walked out.

FIONA. I can't believe you'd do that— (*Rises, crosses to* L. *of sofa.*)

TERESA. No. Well, I haven't actually—

FRANK. Haven't? But I thought you said . . .

TERESA. (*Rises, crosses to* FRANK *and takes his hand.*) I've been thinking it over. You were absolutely right—

FRANK. Was I? Oh—good.

TERESA. After all, why should I give him up? We keep saying it's a love affair but it probably wasn't anything of the sort—

FRANK. Right.

FIONA. Right.

TERESA. Knowing Bob—it's more likely to be some rich old bag he decided to take out just for laughs.

FRANK. (*Amused.*) Rich old bag. Yes—

(FIONA *crosses* U.)

TERESA. You've been a big help. (*Kisses* FRANK.) Thank you, Frank.

FRANK. Not at all. Least I could do.

TERESA. (*Crosses* U., *followed by* FRANK.) Well—I have to run. 'Bye, then.

FIONA. (*Crosses* U.) 'Bye.

TERESA. (*To* FIONA.) Sorry about all this mess.

FIONA. Perfectly alright.

TERESA. You won't mind if I leave you to clean it up, will you? (*Blows* FIONA *a kiss, then goes out.*)

FRANK. Good morning's work.

FIONA. (*Crosses to* FRANK.) Darling, what's going on?

FRANK. (*Crosses to sofa and sits.*) Just a second. This needs a little more thought.

FIONA. Oh? (*Crosses to chair, gets package and purse and crosses* U.) Darling, I bought that dress, by the way.

FRANK. Right.

FIONA. It looks simply ghastly on—

FRANK. Good.

FIONA. But I bought it anyway.

FRANK. Great.

FIONA. I tell you what, I'll put it on. You can tell me what you think. (*Crosses to platform.*)

FRANK. Sure.

FIONA. (*Turns to* FRANK.) Everything alright?

FRANK. Fine.

(FIONA *goes out.* MARY *enters with* BOB's *coffee, puts it down on* PHILLIPS *phone table.*)

MARY. Bob!—Here it is!

(*There is no reply, then* BOB *starts singing in the bath-*

room. FRANK *comes to a decision, rises, looks up number in phone index, crosses to phone, starts dialing.*)

BOB. (*Singing, off.*)
Bless this house, oh Lord, we pray,
Now my wife has gone away.

(MARY *stands for a second, crosses to rocker, dusting.* PHILLIPS' *PHONE RINGS. She looks at it for a moment, glances off, but there's no sign of* BOB. *She answers it uncertainly. She is obviously far from happy using the telephone.*)

MARY. Hello.
FRANK. Hello.
MARY. Hello.
FRANK. Hello. . . . Hello . . .
MARY. Mr. Phillips' residence.
FRANK. Who's this then, the maid?
MARY. No, it's me.
FRANK. Who's me?
MARY. Mary. Mary Detweiler.
FRANK. Mary Detweiler?
MARY. I think Mr. Phillips is in the bathroom at present.
FRANK. Mary Detweiler?
MARY. Who is this talking, please?
FRANK. What are you doing?
MARY. When?
FRANK. Doing there? What are you doing there?
MARY. Dusting.
FRANK. What?
MARY. Dusting. Housework and things. . . .
FRANK. My God . . .
MARY. Beg your pardon?
FRANK. Let me talk to Bob, please?
MARY. I think he's just finished getting dressed.

FRANK. God in heaven.

MARY. Hello. . . . Could you tell me who's calling please?

FRANK. What?

MARY. Could you tell me your name?

FRANK. No. Wrong number. Sorry, wrong number.

MARY. Can I give him any message?

FRANK. No. No. . . .

MARY. Who shall I say phoned?

FRANK. Er . . . Mr. er . . . Mr.—er . . . Mr. Portapram. I'll call back. Good-bye. (*Slams down the phone.*) Good grief.

(BOB *enters with a wraparound towel, and "S" in shaving cream on his bare chest, and a towel around his neck backwards, as Superman.*)

BOB. Who was that?

(FRANK *looks up number in phone index and starts to dial.*)

MARY. (*Stands speechless for a moment, then picks up coffee and Bromo glass and clippings.*) A Mr. Portapram, I think he said. . . .

BOB. What did he want?

MARY. He said he'd call back.

BOB. Never heard of him. Could be my wife's lawyer. Or possibly the editor of the *Village Voice*. (*Goes out, followed by* MARY.)

FRANK. Hello, William Detweiler? . . . Frank Foster here. . . . Yes, good morning to you . . . hope I haven't caught you in the middle of anything. . . . Cleaning your gutters, were you? Good . . . wish I could say the same. . . . Look, listen, William . . . er . . . Mary isn't there with you, is she? . . . Oh . . . no, no, it doesn't matter. . . . You don't happen to know where she is, do you? . . . No, I don't want to talk to her, no . . . I just wondered if you knew where she was, that's all. . . . Yes, probably, probably walking somewhere, yes. . . . Listen, William, something's cropped up here—in the kitchen—yes. . . . You don't happen to know anything about—drain traps, do you . . . ? I seem to be clogged up. . . . Will you? That's very nice of you. Sorry to interrupt your—er—gutter work—but I'd be— About five minutes? Great. Bye-bye. (FIONA *has entered, crossing* D., *displaying her new dress, with tags still hanging from it.* FRANK *hangs up, looks at* FIONA.) Disastrous!

FIONA. I think that's rather brutal, darling.

FRANK. Absolutely disastrous.

FIONA. What if I cut off some of the fringe?

FRANK. At this rate, my whole department could splinter into a dozen pieces. I mean, we've heard of the permissive society . . . but you don't expect to find it running rampant in your own department. (*Crosses* U.) I don't know what's gotten into all of them.

FIONA. (*Crosses* U.) I don't know what you're talking about, darling.

FRANK. All of them. The whole lot. You included. (FIONA *goes toward the door.*) My God, you're not going out again, are you?

FIONA. I thought I'd take this off since you don't like it.

FRANK. I have a little matter to discuss with you. . . .

FIONA. Really?

FRANK. Yes. Sit down . . .

FIONA. (*Slightly apprehensive, crosses* D. R. *of* FOSTER *chair.*) Darling, don't start getting all paternal . . .

FRANK. Sit down, please. (*She sits.*) I think you owe me an explanation. . . . (*Crosses to* FIONA.)

FIONA. Well, I really do have a lot . . .

FRANK. (*Crosses away.*) Wednesday night . . .

FIONA. Wednesday night?

FRANK. Last Wednesday night.

FIONA. Yes?

FRANK. Where were you?

FIONA. I was . . . I was . . . Well, I—I told you.

FRANK. (*Crosses to* FIONA.) You told me you were out with Mary. Mary Detweiler.

FIONA. Oh, did I?

FRANK. Point one. (*Crosses* L.) And I tended to overlook it at the time. When the Detweilers were over here on Thursday, I brought up this so-called meeting to Mary. She said she didn't know anything about it. (*Crosses* U. R. C.)

FIONA. Didn't she?

FRANK. Yes. As I say. I then let the whole thing drop.

FIONA. That's—very decent of you, darling. . . .

FRANK. However, and this is point two, after Terry left this morning I phoned the Phillips' house—and now it's all very clear to me. (*Reaction from* FIONA.) Now I understand what it was you were trying to hide from me Wednesday night. (*Crosses* D. C.) And it's a very serious matter . . .

FIONA. I see.

FRANK. Frankly, I'm very disappointed in you, dear.

FIONA. (*Rises and steps* D. L.) I suppose you must be.

FRANK. Why you should choose to conspire to conceal this rather sordid business from me, I don't know. Deliberately covering up and rather badly at that . . .

FIONA. (*Turns to* FRANK.) I thought . . . you might be hurt, I suppose. . . .

FRANK. Well, I am . . . I am hurt! You've got a label hanging on you, did you know? I am very hurt.

FIONA. Yes, darling.

FRANK. We should be able to share these things, together.

FIONA. Share them?

FRANK. These intimacies?

FIONA. It's not usual, surely . . .

FRANK. (*Crosses to doors.*) I know. You women. Thick as thieves. Well, I think I'll go and put some pants on. . . .

FIONA. What do you want me to do?

FRANK. You? You're dressed all right as you are, aren't you?

FIONA. No, I mean about us.

FRANK. Us? I don't follow you. Make us a little more coffee if you like. That'd be a help. (*Goes out.*)

FIONA. Oh, Lord. (*Goes out into the kitchen.*)

(MARY *appears with a vacuum cleaner and pile of clippings and letters, crosses to desk, puts stack of clippings and letters on desk, bends over to plug in vacuum cleaner. As she does,* TERESA *enters, closes door, turning sign around so that poster side faces audience.* MARY *stands up.*)

MARY. (*Seeing* TERESA.) Hello, Terry.

TERESA. (*Crosses* D. C.) What are you doing here, for heaven's sake? Are you doing daywork now?

MARY. I thought I might be able to help.

TERESA. Help?

MARY. I mean after last night—the soup and all.

TERESA. (*Crosses to desk, unplugs vacuum cleaner, hands cord to* MARY.) Oh, I see. Well, it's very nice of you. I wouldn't do any more, though, this place is a job for life. Jesus, who's messed this up?

MARY. Oh. I think I just straightened . . .

TERESA. (*Picks up stack of clippings.*) Oh, no. They're all mixed up now.

MARY. I'm sorry, have I . . . ?

TERESA. It's just that I had them all sorted out, you see, honey. They're all my press clippings. All the articles I clip out from papers. I had birth control, famine relief and chemical warfare all in separate piles. (FIONA *enters, crosses to phone and dials.*) Now they're all jumbled together.

MARY. I'm terribly sorry.

TERESA. Oh Jesus, all my letters are in here, too.

MARY. Letters?

(PHILLIPS *PHONE RINGS.*)

TERESA. Copies of the ones I send to the editor of the *Voice*, that's all.

MARY. Oh.

(*The PHONE RINGS.* MARY *jumps.*)

TERESA. (*Answering.*) Hello. (FIONA *gives a huge sigh of annoyance.*) PERVERT!

(FIONA *replaces her receiver and exits to kitchen.* TERESA *slams down her receiver and crosses to desk.* BOB *appears in the kitchen doorway.* MARY *sees him first, turns to* TERESA.)

BOB. Well, well, well.

TERESA. Hello. (*They face each other.* MARY *stands, fascinated.*)

BOB. Forget something?

TERESA. No.

BOB. (*Crosses* D. L. *of* C.) Oh. Thought you might have dropped by for your alimony.

TERESA. (*Studying him, crosses toward him.*) You know, deep down inside, you're really rotten, aren't you?

BOB. You should know.

TERESA. Yes, I'm the one that knows!

BOB. Where's Benjy?

TERESA. Asleep.

BOB. Oh. Come here, then.

TERESA. Oh no.

BOB. Come here.

TERESA. No. (*Pause.*) You come here.

(FOSTER *DOOR CHIMES ring.* FIONA *runs to answer it.* BOB *takes a step toward* TERESA, *who draws her arm back and starts to punch him. He grabs her arm and throws her over his shoulder, turning.* MARY *has been watching, riveted, all this while.*)

BOB. You stupid bitch. (*Crosses toward kitchen door.* TERESA *is hitting* BOB *on the back with her fists.*)

TERESA. Dirty bastard. (*Just before they go into kitchen—to* MARY.) Honey, you won't wake Benjamin, will you? (*They exit.*)

(MARY *begins putting the cord back on vacuum cleaner as* FIONA *enters with* WILLIAM, *who brandishes a monkey wrench.*)

WILLIAM. Came over as quickly as I could. . . . (*Crosses* D.) This will do the trick. (*Waves wrench.*)
FIONA. Oh?
WILLIAM. Have you fixed up in no time.
FIONA. (*Crosses to coffee table, picks up cup and saucer.*) Good. Thank you. (*Pause.*) My husband won't be a minute.
WILLIAM. Ah. Coping with the emergency, is he?
FIONA. Well, he's just putting on some trousers.
WILLIAM. Oh, I see. Hope I haven't called at an inconvenient time.

(MARY *crosses with vacuum cleaner and exits into* PHILLIPS' *kitchen.*)

FIONA. No, not at all. Sit down, William. (*Crosses to sofa table, puts down cup and saucer.* WILLIAM *sits.*)
WILLIAM. I'd like to take this opportunity to thank you on behalf of myself and Mrs. Detweiler for a delightful dinner the other evening.
FIONA. Thank you.
WILLIAM. Thank *you*. (*A pause.* FIONA *smiles awkwardly at* WILLIAM. *He smiles back.*) That's a very attractive dress, if I may say so.
FIONA. Oh. Do you think so? Thank you.
WILLIAM. And brand-new today, unless I'm very mistaken.
FIONA. Yes?
WILLIAM. I spotted the label. . . .
FIONA. Oh yes.

WILLIAM. Overlooked it, didn't you?

FIONA. No, I left it on deliberately. . . .

WILLIAM. Oh?

FIONA. I've tried it without, but I've come to the conclusion that I prefer the dress with the label on. (*Crosses and picks up timer off coffee table.*)

WILLIAM. Oh. I'm sorry.

FIONA. (*Crosses, puts timer on sofa table.*) That's alright. I wonder if you could tell me something.

WILLIAM. I'll try my best.

FIONA. (*Crosses between chair and sofa.*) I want to ask you a theoretical question. It's purely theoretical, mind you. I just want to know how you'd react.

WILLIAM. O.K. Fire away.

FIONA. If you found out that your wife was having an affair with another man, how would you react?

WILLIAM. What a question.

FIONA. Yes, it is, isn't it?

WILLIAM. I mean, Mary would never dream of it. . . .

FIONA. Of course not; I said it's theoretical.

WILLIAM. I see. (*Considers.*) Well . . .

FIONA. I mean, for instance, do you think you'd say . . . "I'm rather disappointed in you. You might have shared it with me." Something like that?

WILLIAM. No. I don't think I'd say that. Hit her . . . perhaps? (FIONA *crosses* R. *of sofa.*) Sorry I can't be more help. I haven't had any real experience in that kind of situation.

FIONA. No, neither have I. . . .

FRANK. (*Entering.*) Ah. (FIONA *crosses above sofa.*) Hello there, William. Thanks for coming by. (*Crossing to bar.*)

WILLIAM. (*Rises, crosses* R. *of chair.*) I was just saying . . . I came as soon as I could.

FRANK. I'm glad you did. First of all, let's have a drink . . . and then we have to sit down and talk.

FIONA. (*Crosses to* U.) Yes, well, I'll just go upstairs, darling, and . . .

FRANK. No, no, no. We need you right here with us. Sit down.

FIONA. Well, I really . . .

FRANK. Sit down. You've got to have a drink. (FIONA *sits in armchair*.) We've all got to have a drink. . . .

WILLIAM. (*Puts cup on coffee table*.) Well, it's a little early, but still . . .

FRANK. I absolutely insist. (*Hands* FIONA, *then* WILLIAM, *a drink*.) Here we are.

WILLIAM. Thanks very much.

FRANK. (*Crossing to bar, picks up his drink, crosses* U. L. *of chair*.) Now then. Let's get down to cases. William . . .

WILLIAM. Right . . . drain trap . . .

FRANK. What?

WILLIAM. The one I came over to look at.

FRANK. Oh, that drain trap. Yes, well, that's the first thing, William.

WILLIAM. What is?

FRANK. There is no drain trap.

WILLIAM. But I thought . . .

FRANK. I'm afraid you thought incorrectly. The drain trap was just an excuse to get you over here.

WILLIAM. Why?

FIONA. Darling, what is going on?

FRANK. Please. . . . I'm afraid, William, that what I have to say will come as somewhat of a shock. I'm sorry to say that my wife has been deceiving me—that's why I asked her to stay here so that she can tell you about the whole sordid affair from start to finish.

FIONA. (*Smiles at* WILLIAM, *looks at* FRANK, *rises uncomfortably, turns to* FRANK.) You can't be serious!

FRANK. Hmm?

FIONA. You expect me to sit here calmly, and tell— William everything? Is that what you're getting at?

FRANK. That's the general idea, yes—

FIONA. And just what are you trying to do—humiliate me? (*Crosses* D. L.)

FRANK. No, dear. William has the right to know.

FIONA. (*Crosses above rocker.*) William has the right to know? Oh well, in that case, invite the mailman in. Invite the butcher . . . if you really want to humiliate me, why not make a real show of it?

FRANK. What's the butcher got to do with it?

(WILLIAM *crosses* U. C.)

FIONA. (*Crossing to* FRANK.) I think this is sinking very low. At least if you hit me that would show you cared. (*Crosses to bar, puts drink on bar.*) Go on. Hit me! Hit me!

FRANK. What's gotten into you? Are you overheated from the hair dryer?

FIONA. Don't try to be funny with me!

WILLIAM. (*Puts drink on sofa table, crosses in to* FRANK.) Pardon me, I'm not sure . . .

FIONA. The point is, William, my husband is trying to tell you, in a rather sordid way, about a very silly, very trivial love affair between Bob Phillips and . . .

FRANK. And your wife, William. Exactly. (FIONA *turns and collapses on bar with great relief.*) I think you could have put it a little better than that. I was trying to spare the man's feelings.

WILLIAM. My wife?

FRANK. Sorry, William. You had to know sooner or later.

FIONA. His wife? (*Crosses below rocker.*) You mean Mary Detweiler?

FRANK. (*Crossing* D. L. C.) Of course I mean Mary Detweiler. He only has one wife, hasn't he? I hope.

WILLIAM. (*Crosses to* FRANK.) My wife and Bob Phillips?

FIONA. Darling, you can't mean it? (*Crosses to* FRANK.) Bob Phillips and Mary Detweiler?

FRANK. Mary Detweiler and Bob Phillips. I wish everyone wouldn't keep repeating the same damn thing. . . .

FIONA. (*Crosses to bar.*)   WILLIAM. (*Crosses* R.)
That's   utterly   ridicu-   I've never heard anything
lous. . . .   so . . . absurd. . . .

FRANK. Yes, I know it must be quite a blow to you,
William. (*Turns to* FIONA.) I don't know why you're so
surprised all of a sudden, darling. You've been covering
up for the poor girl for the past three days. . . .

FIONA. Covering up?

WILLIAM. (*Crosses to* FRANK.) Absolutely absurd. . . .

FRANK. Now let's be completely fair about this,
William. You haven't been exactly innocent yourself, have
you? There isn't much that escapes me, so don't try to
deny it. I know this is not the moment to remind you of
your own exploits in those boots. . . . (*Crosses* R. *of*
WILLIAM.)

WILLIAM. Boots?

FRANK. The ones you keep on the filing cabinet. I know
all about those, too, you see. . . .

WILLIAM. Those are my clamming boots. . . .

FRANK. I don't care what you call it, William. (*Crosses*
U. L. *of chair.*) I just want to deal perfectly calmly with
the facts. Last Wednesday night my wife returned home
very late and informed me that she had been spending
the evening with Mary. This, I have since discovered, was
palpably untrue.

FIONA. Darling, you've gotten hold of the most . . .

FRANK. Shh, please! May I just . . . This story was
my wife's invention.

WILLIAM. Was it, Mrs. Foster?

FIONA. Well, in a way, yes, but I—

FRANK. You see.

FIONA. But I certainly wasn't covering up for Mary . . .

FRANK. What other possible reason could you have had
for concocting this story? Answer me that?

FIONA. (*Stumped.*) Well . . . none at all. (*Crosses
above* PHILLIPS *chair to sofa.*)

FRANK. Right. I'm afraid you've lost the ball game,
sweetheart.

WILLIAM. But I can't see that that proves . . .

FRANK. I'm coming to that, William. This morning, I had Teresa Phillips over here. She told me she discovered her husband was having an affair. When she left, I phoned Bob Phillips. I spoke to your wife, William. She was in his house. . . .

WILLIAM. At Bob Phillips'! What was she doing at Bob Phillips'!

(*Long pause.*)

FRANK. (*Crosses* D. L.) I'm trying to spell this out in words of one syllable, William. She answered the phone, pretending to be the maid or something. She informed me Phillips was upstairs in the bathroom. She claimed to be dusting. (*Turns to* WILLIAM.) You can put whatever interpretation on that you like. To me it only pointed to one thing . . .

WILLIAM. (*Dazed, incredulous.*) I—can't believe this. . . . My wife? (*Crosses* R. *of* C.) Is this true, Mrs. Foster?

FIONA. I . . . um . . . mmmm. (*Sits.*)

WILLIAM. Of course. That's what you were trying to tell me before your husband came in, wasn't it? How would you react, you said, if you found your wife had been unfaithful to you? And I said . . .

FIONA. You'd hit her . . . yes, I remember.

WILLIAM. Yes. Did I say that? Yes, that's right. . . . (*Crosses to* FIONA. FRANK *steps in.*)

FRANK. Easy now, feller—

WILLIAM. Could I possibly have a drink, please—

FRANK. Yes, of course, of course. (*Crosses to bar— turns to* WILLIAM.) What would you like? A Bloody Mary? No. No. Sorry. (*Pours a Scotch.*)

FIONA. (*Rises.*) William, I really would think before you do anything . . .

WILLIAM. Do you realize, Mrs. Foster, the hours I've put into that woman? When I met her, you know, she was nothing. Nothing at all. (*Crosses* R.) With my own hands I built her up. Encouraging her to join the Book of the Month Club . . . (*Crosses* L.) . . . I introduced her to the Concert Classics Record Club . . . I've coaxed her, encouraged her to think . . . perhaps even bullied her . . . (FRANK *steps in.*) . . . some might say. (*Taking Scotch.*) Thank you very much. (*Crosses* R.) Her taste in clothes was terrible, my own mother encouraged her towards adventurous cooking . . . everything. I've done everything.

FIONA. Good for you. Cheers.

(WILLIAM *gulps drink.*)

FRANK. Hey. Watch it.

WILLIAM. And then a man like Phillips . . . Phillips can come along and . . . How dare he? How dare he? (*Hands* FRANK *glass.*)

FRANK. Might be a good idea if you stayed for lunch, William.

WILLIAM. How dare he . . .

FIONA. William, dear, do sit down . . .

WILLIAM. HOW DARE HE . . . (*Rushes out.*)

(FRANK *crosses* U. FIONA *crosses to* FRANK *and takes glass.*)

FIONA. Stop him!

(FRANK *rushes out. Comes right back in.*)

FRANK. Too late. (*Crosses to phone, looks up number in phone index.*)

FIONA. Now look what you've done.

FRANK. Me? (*Starts dialing.*)

FIONA. (*Crosses to bar.*) You realize that man is in an unbalanced state. (*Crosses to platform.*) The mood he's in at the moment, he could shoot someone.

FRANK. With a monkey wrench? Do you think that's possible? I'm calling Bob Phillips and warn him.

FIONA. They were perfectly happy until you started in on them.

FRANK. Me?

(MARY *enters with coat on, crosses to* PHILLIPS *front door.*)

FIONA. Yes.

FRANK. Now look here, I really don't think you can keep blaming me for this.

FIONA. I'm going to change. I'm going to get out of this monstrosity. (*Goes out.*)

(PHILLIPS *phone rings.* MARY *turns from door, which she has left ajar. She answers it.*)

MARY. Hello.

FRANK. Hello.

MARY. Hello. Oh, hello, this is Mr. Portapram, isn't it?

FRANK. No. Is that you, Mary, now . . .

MARY. I'm sorry, Mr. Portapram, Mr. Phillips is in the bedroom right . . .

FRANK. Mary . . .

MARY. His wife is with him, so I don't like to disturb them. . . .

FRANK. The three of them—it's getting worse. Mary, listen to me. This is Foster, do you hear? Foster . . .

MARY. Who?

FRANK. Frank Foster . . .

MARY. Oh, I thought you were Mr. . . .

FRANK. Yes, yes, of course. But I'm not. I'm me. Now listen, Mary. This is urgent. You must hang up the phone and leave that house immediately, do you understand?

MARY. Yes. But—

FRANK. Don't argue. Just do as you're told. But before you leave you must go upstairs and tell Phillips to lock himself in that bedroom and stay there. . . .

MARY. But I can't go in, he's with his wife. . . .

FRANK. This is a matter of life and death, woman. Now, Mary, when you've done that, leave the house. But whatever you do, don't go to your home. Come over to my house. And run, run all the way, do you hear?

MARY. But, Mr. Foster, I've to get William's dinner. He gets so grumpy . . .

FRANK. William is more than grumpy right now, Mary, he's . . .

WILLIAM. (*Entering.*) MARY! (*Shuts door and leans against it.*)

MARY. Oh, speak of the devil, Mr. Foster. Here he is . . .

FRANK. Take cover! Take cover! Get down on the floor. (*Gets down on floor.*)

MARY. Beg your pardon?

WILLIAM. So it's true, Mary. It's true. (*Crosses above sofa to R. and below during the following dialogue.*)

MARY. What?

FRANK. Mary, Mary . . . for goodness' sake . . . (*Realizing he is talking to no one.*)

WILLIAM. (*Simultaneously with* FRANK.) I would not have believed this of you, Mary. I would never have believed it. How could you do this? (*Loudly.*) How could you do this? (*Crosses U. L. to* PHILLIPS *kitchen door.*)

MARY. You aren't upset that I came over here, are you, William?

FRANK. Mary, get hold of a blunt instrument.

WILLIAM. (*Pushes up sweater sleeves, starts to roll up shirt sleeves.*) Leave this house! Leave this house, this instant. . . .

MARY. But I'm on the telephone. . . . (*Starts gnawing her nails.*)

WILLIAM. (*Crossing to* MARY.) I am warning you, Mary. I am very near to violence. (*Smacks her hand.*) I have never struck or molested you since the day we were married. Even under these circumstances I don't want to start. But I will, Mary, I will . . . if you do not leave this house . . . (*Crosses to* D. L.)

MARY. I only came over to help . . .

WILLIAM. Help?

MARY. She's been having a love affair . . .

WILLIAM. Who has?

MARY. Terry. With a man from the newspaper.

FRANK. My God, another one.

MARY. Just a minute, Mr. Foster.

FRANK. Mary . . .

MARY. She writes to him. He's the editor of the *Village Voice* . . . Bob told me.

WILLIAM. What a feeble, miserable story. (*Advancing on her.*) You wanton slut!

FRANK. Hello!

(BOB *enters in his dressing gown.*)

BOB. Look, I'd be grateful if you two would take your domestic quarrels somewhere else. . . .

WILLIAM. (*Leaps forward and swings a blow at* BOB *and catches him in the stomach.*) You swine, Phillips. You swine.

BOB. (*Collapsing on his knees with a grunt.*) Aagh!

WILLIAM. That'll teach you!

MARY. William!

WILLIAM. That'll teach you!

FRANK. Hello! Hello!

(FIONA *enters and closes both doors.* WILLIAM *paces back and forth between* MARY *and* BOB.)

FIONA. Hello.

FRANK. Get down on the floor, dear.

(FIONA *crosses above sofa to the* R. *of sofa.*)

FIONA. Darling, what's the matter?

FRANK. No shots yet, thank God, but . . .
WILLIAM. I warn you, if you get up, I'll hit you **again**, Phillips.
BOB. What the hell was that for . . . ?
MARY. William, are you alright?
FIONA. Darling, are you alright?
WILLIAM. I'm alright.
FRANK. I'm alright.

(TERESA *enters.*)

WILLIAM. I'm the only one in this house that is alright. . . . (*Crosses* L.)

(BOB *starts to get up.* WILLIAM *hits him in the right eye.*
MARY, *still holding the phone, screams.* FRANK, *at
sound of scream, yells and jumps back.* FIONA, *reacting to this—cries out.* BOB *collapses, falls against
*D. *side of* PHILLIPS *kitchen door.* TERESA *turns, hits*
WILLIAM *in stomach and he doubles over.* TERESA
gives WILLIAM *a karate chop and he falls behind the*
FOSTER *chair.* TERESA *crosses to* BOB *and comforts
him. When* TERESA *hits* WILLIAM, MARY *screams
again, drops phone, turns and runs out* PHILLIPS *door
and immediately bursts through* FOSTER *door.* FRANK
and FIONA *whirl round, taken completely by surprise.*)

MARY. Aaaah. . . . Aaah. (*Falls in a dead faint.*)

CURTAIN

ACT TWO

SCENE 2

The same. Sunday morning. FRANK *is* D. L.

FRANK. Fellow workers . . . members of my department . . . (*Crosses to coffee table.*) Let's put our cards on the table. . . .

(FIONA *enters with two coffee cups, crosses* D. R. *of sofa.*)

FIONA. Coffee?
FRANK. Just one cup. . . . Oh, thank you.
FIONA. Are you sure this is the right thing?
FRANK. Absolutely.
FIONA. But it really has nothing to do with us. (*Crosses* C.)
FRANK. They're all members of my department. As such I feel their physical and to a certain extent spiritual welfare are my concern. (*Puts cup down.*)
FIONA. Oh, darling, that's awfully pompous. (*Sits in* FOSTER *chair.*)
FRANK. There is nothing pompous about human concern. I wonder if you'd mind not sitting there. (*Crosses* L. *of chair.*) I plan to take the chair at my own meeting. Where's Mary?
FIONA. (*Rises, crosses to sofa and sits.*) I just woke her up. She had a good long rest, the best thing for her.
FRANK. As long as she's down for the meeting . . .
FIONA. She'll be down. Probably starving too. She didn't eat anything last night. Not a bite.

(*The DOORBELL RINGS.*)

FRANK. (*Crosses* D. L.) That'll be Phillips.
FIONA. (*Rises.*) I'll let them in. I hope this isn't going to take too long. I've put newspaper down in the hall, so their baby can drool its little head off . . . (*Goes out.*)

FRANK. (*Muttering.*) Teammates—a team that plays together stays together, but some of us have been playing too hard. . . . I suppose some of you are wondering why I . . . (FIONA, BOB *and* TERESA *enter on platform.*) Here we are. (*Turns, crosses* U. FRANK, *shaking* BOB's *hand.*) Come in.

BOB. Hi, Frank.

FRANK. (*Shaking* TERESA's *hand.*) Come in.

TERESA. Hello, Frank.

FRANK. (*Shaking* FIONA's *hand.*) Come in. (*Crosses* D. L. *of* FOSTER *chair.*) Please sit down. (TERESA *crosses to sofa, sits on right end.* BOB *crosses to* FRANK.) Sit down. Sit down. Now I've asked you here . . .

FIONA. (*Calls.*) Mary!

BOB. What's it all about?

FRANK. Well, I've asked you . . .

FIONA. I'll bring you some coffee. (*Goes out to kitchen.*)

FRANK. I've asked . . . (*Noticing* BOB's *bruised face.*) That's a nasty bump, Bob. Where'd you get that?

BOB. That's an interesting story, actually. . . .

TERESA. William did it. . . .

FRANK. William? I see.

BOB. More than we do. (*Sits in armchair.*)

FRANK. Exactly. Bob, would you mind not sitting . . . (BOB *rises, crosses to sofa and sits on left end of sofa.*) Thank you. Now, the idea of this morning is to try and undo some of the damage . . .

(FIONA *enters; to sofa table with a coffee tray with four cups.*)

FIONA. Coffee? Bob? Terry?

BOB. Thanks.

TERESA. Thank you.

FRANK. The point is, Terry . . .

FIONA. Terry, cream?

TERESA. No.

FRANK. Terry . . .

FIONA. Sugar?

TERESA. No, thank you.

FRANK. Terry! Let's keep calm, shall we? I warned you on the phone that we may be in for some shocks. . . .

FIONA. (*Crosses behind* R. *of sofa, hands* TERESA *coffee.*) You're both looking terribly well. . . .

(FRANK *crosses* D. L. *and back.*)

TERESA. Are we?

FIONA. (*Crosses back to sofa table.*) I love your bruise, Bob. . . . How did you get it?

BOB. Oh, I . . . picked it up fairly cheap somewhere. . . .

FIONA. (*Handing* BOB *his coffee.*) You look good in it. I'd keep it.

FRANK. I have to insist that we keep to the subject. We have a lot to get through this morning. . . .

BOB. This has the air of a kind of third-rate stockholders' meeting. Where exactly do Terry and I come into it?

FRANK. That's a pretty cynical thing to say, Bob. Considering.

TERESA. Oh, what have you been doing now?

BOB. Me?

TERESA. Yes.

BOB. Nothing.

FRANK. Will you please address your remarks to the chair. (FIONA *crosses to* FIONA *chair and sits.* FRANK *crosses to* BOB.) Now, Bob, before Mary comes down, and before William gets here . . .

BOB. (*Rises.*) William!

FRANK. Please sit down, Bob.

BOB. I'm not staying here. That man's unbalanced.

FRANK. I wouldn't go so far as to say unbalanced. I agree what he did was drastic, but, under the circumstances, it was understandable.

BOB. Oh, perfectly understandable. He's off his nut, that's all. (*Sits.*)

FRANK. (*Crosses* U. *to* L. *of armchair.*) Darling, would you mind not . . . (FIONA *rises, crosses* U.) Now before Mary comes down, and before . . .

(MARY *enters.*)

FIONA. Ah. Here she is. Mary, come in and sit down. . . . (*Crosses to sofa table.*)

MARY. Hello.

TERESA. Hello, Mary.

FRANK. Sit down, Mary. (MARY *sits in* FOSTER *armchair.*) No, not there, Mary, please!

(MARY *rises.* BOB *rises.* MARY *crosses, sits in* C. *of sofa.* BOB *sits.*)

FIONA. Coffee, Mary?

MARY. Thank you.

FRANK. I was just saying, Mary, that the reason we're all here is that we want to try to straighten things out for you. . . .

FIONA. (*Handing* MARY *coffee.*) Mary . . .

MARY. Thank you.

FRANK. Not at all. The point is, that when William gets here . . .

MARY. William! (*Rises.*) Oh, no . . .

FRANK. Oh, please sit down, Mary. You're perfectly safe.

MARY. I don't think I can . . . (*Sits.*)

FRANK. When William gets here, you must be absolutely straight and honest with him. Don't try and pretend it's anything other than what it is . . . a love affair . . . a perfectly simple love affair between yourself and Bob Phillips.

MARY. (*Rises.*) A what?

BOB. Eh?

TERESA. What?

FRANK. (*A bit startled by their reaction.*) Well, those are the facts, aren't they?

BOB. (*Crosses to* FRANK.) Frank. You must be joking.

FRANK. I don't think it's anything to joke about. . . .

MARY. I haven't had an affair with Bob . . . honestly, Terry.

TERESA. (*Laughing.*) No, I believe you.

FRANK. Well, in that case I . . . (*Crosses to* MARY.) Are you sure you haven't?

BOB. Where the hell did you get that idea . . .

FRANK. Um. Well, it . . . it came in dribs and drabs. Oh well, if you haven't had an affair—that changes the whole agenda. (*Crosses* D. L.) It certainly makes things a lot simpler . . .

(*The* FOSTER *DOORBELL RINGS.*)

MARY. William!

FIONA. Oh Lord. (*Goes to answer the door.*)

BOB. Is that why he hit me?

FRANK. Obviously. . . .

BOB. It's always nice to know . . . (*Crosses to sofa.*) . . . when you're knocked down in your own living room.

TERESA. You'd be terrific in a crisis. You didn't even put up a fight.

BOB. (*Sits.*) I didn't even know there was a fight.

(WILLIAM *enters, followed by* FIONA.)

WILLIAM. I came over as quickly as I could. (*Crosses to* FRANK, *followed by* FIONA, *and* FIONA *crosses to sofa table.*) I don't know too much about immersion heaters but I'll see what . . . Oh . . . (*Glares at the assembled company.*)

FRANK. Ah, William.

BOB. Hello.

WILLIAM. Is this a practical joke?

FRANK. William . . .

WILLIAM. It's not very funny. Inviting me over here and then confronting me with *him* and *her*. . . . Do you think I want to sit down in the same room with *them* . . .

FRANK. William . . .

WILLIAM. I have a blinding headache, and I was u' half the night with one. . . . I came here in good faith t have a look at the thermostat on your immersion heate . . . as you asked me . . .

FRANK. WILLIAM!

WILLIAM. (*Startled.*) Yes, sir!

FRANK. (*Crosses down.* WILLIAM *follows.*) There's been a misunderstanding, William.

BOB. Yes, you could call it that.

FRANK. The point is . . . er . . . I think I misinformed you . . .

WILLIAM. What about?

BOB. About Mary and me.

FRANK. (*Laughing.*) My information was inaccurate.

WILLIAM. You mean . . . ? (BOB *shakes his head.* MARY *shakes her head.*) I see.

FIONA. (*Crosses* D. *between sofa and* PHILLIPS *chair.*) William, I suggest the best thing you can do is to take Mary home and have a nice lunch together and then you can both kiss and make up. . . . (*Crosses to* U. *doors.*) I'll see you all out.

(TERESA *rises, crosses in front of* BOB *onto the platform.* BOB *crosses* U. WILLIAM *crosses* U.)

WILLIAM. Well, I don't know just what to say. I've been pretty badly misinformed. (BOB *and* WILLIAM *are below platform.*)

BOB. You should have checked your facts first, shouldn't you?

WILLIAM. Well . . . Bob. I hope you weren't too badly hurt?

BOB. (*Crosses out foyer.*) Not too badly at all. Few days in an iron lung and I'll be fine.

TERESA. How's your head?

WILLIAM. Not too bad, I . . .

TERESA. (*Crosses out to foyer.*) Sorry about that, too.

WILLIAM. No, no. My fault. . . . Well, I think the best thing is for us both to leave now . . . rather than . . .

MARY. Yes?

WILLIAM. (*Crosses to* MARY.) Come on, let's go.

MARY. Just a minute . . .

WILLIAM. Yes?

MARY. What about me? You apologized to everybody else, what about me?

WILLIAM. I don't have to apologize to you. I was misinformed.

MARY. How?

WILLIAM. You must have understood the situation. I was told . . .

MARY. You always told me not to believe everything people tell you. . . .

WILLIAM. True, but . . .

MARY. Then why did you?

WILLIAM. The situation is entirely different. . . . Mr. Foster told me . . .

MARY. I want an apology . . .

WILLIAM. Mary, let's not make a scene here. . . .

MARY. I'm not leaving here till I get an apology.

WILLIAM. Darling, I'm going to get angry. . . .

BOB. Go on—apologize.

WILLIAM. Do you mind?

TERESA. I think you owe her an apology, William. . . .

WILLIAM. Thank you very much, Terry, I'll deal with my own affairs.

FRANK. Apologize, William. It's easier that way.

WILLIAM. Oh. Well—if you say so, Mr. Foster. . . . In that case, I'm a . . . I'm a . . . I'm a . . . (*Can't say it.*)

MARY. (*Rises, crosses to* WILLIAM.) Thank you. That'll do. We'll go now. (*Crosses to* FRANK.) Mrs. Foster, Mr. Foster, thank you very much for looking after me. . . .

FIONA. Our pleasure.

FRANK. Good-bye, Mary. . . . Good to see you. . . .

MARY. William?

WILLIAM. (*Crosses to below doors. Continues spluttering and gesticulating, unable to say anything.*) Uh— (*Exits,* FIONA *follows.*)

MARY. (*In doorway, indicating the departed* WILLIAM.) It's very difficult for him. You see, he's never been wrong before. (*As* MARY *goes out,* FIONA *enters.*)

FIONA. Oh, Terry, your baby seems to be eating all that newspaper. Is it good for him?

TERESA. Depends which one. (FIONA *and* TERESA *exit.*)

FRANK. Bob, a word of warning.

BOB. (*Crosses to* FRANK.) What?

FRANK. When Mary was here last night, I couldn't get much out of her, but she did say something I think you ought to know. . . . Apparently, Terry may be getting herself involved with some . . . newspaperman . . .

BOB. Newspaperman?

FRANK. Yes, apparently. . . .

BOB. You mean one of those guys who stand on corners shouting . . .

FRANK. No, no, a journalist. . . .

BOB. Oh. Really? Thanks. . . .

FRANK. Just watch out.

BOB. (*Puzzled.*) Yes, right. (*Turns and crosses up on platform.*) See you, then.

FRANK. Right, get the team back on the field tomorrow. At full strength.

BOB. Full strength. (*Goes out.*)

FRANK. (*Pleased, crosses to sofa and sits,* L.) Good . . . good . . . good. . . .

(FIONA *returns, crosses to coffee table, picks up two cups and saucers.*)

FIONA. Well done, darling.

FRANK. I'd say that was a good morning's work. A good morning's work.

FIONA. (*Crosses to sofa table.*) That's really the most awful baby. It left a damp patch on the carpet again. I'll have to leave the front door open . . . to let it dry out. . . . (*Begins to stack up the coffee cups.*)

FRANK. (*Thoughtful suddenly.*) Just a minute. There's something missing. There's a loose end here somewhere. . . .

FIONA. (*Crosses to coffee table, gets cups.*) Yes, well, don't you worry about that now. You spend much too much time worrying about other people's problems. . . . (*Crosses to sofa table.*)

FRANK. First, you told me that you were out with Mary last Wednesday. . . .

FIONA. Did I?

FRANK. Yes. Then you said, under pressure, "No, I was just covering up for Mary," didn't you?

FIONA. Yes, possibly. . . .

FRANK. However, since Mary was not having an affair, you didn't have to cover up for her, did you?

FIONA. I suppose not. . . .

FRANK. So the question still remains . . . what were you up to on Wednesday night . . . ?

FIONA. Oh, I was . . . doing this and that. . . .

FRANK. You've been acting peculiarly lately.

FIONA. Really?

FRANK. Yes.

FIONA. Good. More coffee?

FRANK. Where were you?

FIONA. You don't really want to know . . . do you?

FRANK. (*Turns to* FIONA.) Yes, I do.

FIONA. Oh. (*Pause.*) Well. Well, I did something rather . . . silly. . . . (*Pause.* FIONA *crosses* L. *of sofa.*)

FRANK. Did you?

FIONA. Yes. (*Pause.*) Are you going to be very angry with me?

FRANK. No.

FIONA. Well, we sort of met and then he . . . well, we both—

FRANK. Another man . . . ?

FIONA. Yes.

FRANK. Oh.

FIONA. It really wasn't anything.

FRANK. No. Do I know him?

FIONA. Sort of.

FRANK. I see.

FIONA. (*Crosses behind* FRANK.) It really wasn't . . . I mean . . . anything. . . . He was really nothing compared to you. (*Embracing* FRANK.)

FRANK. Oh.

FIONA. Will you forgive me?

FRANK. Yes, of course. I mean, nothing much else I can do, is there?

FIONA. (*Kissing him on top of the head.*) Darling.

FRANK. Hmmmm.

FIONA. I'll tell you what I'll do. I'll make us a special non-anniversary dinner to make up for it. Something divine. And you can open a bottle of wine and we'll get crocked. Hmmm?

FRANK. Um?

FIONA. I know, I'll put on some of that delicious perfume you bought me and we'll have an orgy. How about that?

FRANK. Oh, yes. Do that!

FIONA. (*Moving off with cups to kitchen.*) Good.

FRANK. Fiona, who was it?

FIONA. (*Off.*) Who?

FRANK. This man you . . . ?

FIONA. (*Off.*) Oh. Nobody important at all. . . .

FRANK. Somebody we know, though . . . ?

FIONA. (*Off.*) It really doesn't matter. . . .

FRANK. (*Muttering.*) Somebody we know . . . ? (*Picks up phone index, puts it on coffee table, starts to go through it.*) Adams . . . no—Atkinson . . . no—Associated Dairies . . . no— (*Continues to mutter.*)

(TERESA *and* BOB *enter their house, laughing.*)

TERESA. (*Crosses* D. C., *then* L. *to rocker.*) What a waste of a morning!

BOB. (*Crosses* D. C.) I'm sure Frank enjoyed it. . . .

TERESA. (*Laughing.*) You and Mary Detweiler . . . I'd love to have seen that. . . .

BOB. I don't know how the hell Frank got that idea. . . . (*They laugh.* BOB *sits in armchair.*)

TERESA. Now if he'd said you and Fiona? Is it all over between you? (*Sits, rocker.*)

BOB. (*Rises, crosses to* TERESA.) What?

TERESA. It was pretty obvious.

BOB. Oh. (*Crosses* U.)

TERESA. Well, if it had to be someone, I'd rather it was her than Mary. . . .

BOB. So would I.

TERESA. No, I mean, Mary's a real clinger. If she wanted you, she'd hang on. Fiona knows which side her bread is buttered on.

FRANK. Yates . . . Yeoman . . . YMCA . . . (*Doubles take toward kitchen.* TERESA *opens bottle of perfume.*)

BOB. What's that?

TERESA. (*Hands him perfume.*) Perfume. It was on the hall table at Fiona's. Benjamin must have reached out and taken it. . . .

BOB. Oh, yes?

TERESA. I think I'll keep it. I think she owes it to me. Don't see what you saw in her—unless it was a promotion.

BOB. (*Crosses to chair and sits.*) Come on. What about you?

TERESA. Me?

BOB. Your friend. The newspaperman.

TERESA. Newspaperman?

BOB. I've heard.

TERESA. I don't know any newspaperman.

BOB. No?

TERESA. No. I wish I did. You know you were crazy to do it. Frank has to find out sooner or later.

FRANK. Somebody we know? . . . Ah! Good God! Good God! Yes, of course! (*The realization dawns, and then he picks up the phone, looks up number in index and dials.*)

(BOB *crosses to kitchen.*)

TERESA. Where are you going?

BOB. (*Dignified.*) I'm going to make us lunch.

TERESA. You're what?

BOB. I'm going to make us some goddamned lunch. What's wrong with that? (*Exits.*)

TERESA. (*Amused.*) Nothing. That's lovely. (*Starts to follow him.*) My God!! (*After a long pause,* TERESA's *phone rings.* FRANK *is growling menacingly into the phone.* TERESA *advances, warily, and picks up the phone, and hears* FRANK *growling.*) This is screwdriver, isn't it?

FRANK. Screwdriver?

TERESA. Oh, good, you're talking. That's a big step forward. No, listen to me. Does it give you some sort of kick telephoning women and trying to frighten them? Does it?

FRANK. Er—no—not really. I don't think so. I don't really know.

TERESA. Look. You obviously need help. Haven't you got *anyone* you can talk to . . . a wife or a mother . . .

FRANK. Mother's passed away . . .

BOB. (*Entering, wearing apron.*) Where the hell are the frying pans?

TERESA. (*To* BOB.) Sssh!

FRANK. (*As* FIONA *enters, misinterpreting. Whispers.*) . . . and my wife's in the kitchen. . . .

FIONA. What's that?

FRANK. (*To* FIONA.) Sssh!

TERESA. Look, I'm sorry to sound technical, but . . . are you . . . very frustrated?

BOB. (*Crosses to* L. *of* TERESA.) Eh?

TERESA. Ssssh!

FRANK. Frustrated?

TERESA. You know. Sexually.

FRANK. (*Looks at* FIONA, *then back to phone.*) Sexually?

FIONA. (*Crosses in.*) Sexually?

FRANK. Shhh!

TERESA. Look. I can't talk any more now but if you'd like to, call me again sometime and we can even meet somewhere and have a session.

FRANK. Meet somewhere . . . yes . . . that'd be nice. . . .

TERESA. Good. Well, you've got my number, so call me up any time you like.

FRANK. Thank you very much. I'll do that. Good-bye.

TERESA. Good-bye. (*They laugh.*)

BOB. Who was that?

FIONA. Who was that?

TERESA. (*Pleased.*) Someone who needs my help.

FRANK. Just a kid I went to school with. . . .

CURTAIN

PROPERTY PLOT

Radio
Calendar
Rolltop desk
Clippings
Mug with pencils
Paperback book
Telephone book
Scissors
Typewriter
Stack of clippings and
  letters clipped together
Letters
Envelopes
Paper clips
Newspapers
Memo pad
Wastebasket
Magazine rack with
  magazines and papers
Squeaker toy
Window blind
Sofa
End table
Sofa table
Coffee table
Radio
Letter opener
Ashtray, glass
White phone
Memo pad
Pencil
Address index
Timer
Silver cigarette box
Crystal ashtray
Armchair, blue
Phone table
Phone
Armchair, yellow

Rocker
Stack toy
Drapes
Bar
Decanter
3 bottles of Scotch
1 small soda
1 small ginger ale
1 small tonic
2 jars with fake avocado
  plants
2 pots artificial flowers
Bamboo window blind
1 bottle bourbon
3 china plates
2 crystal decanters
2 sets of fake books
Assorted bar accessories
2 small blue vases
Small girl figurine
Large oriental plant
2 small crystal bud vases
2 wineglasses
3 martini glasses
2 old-fashioned glasses
Iron, ceramic
Silver ice bucket
Martini pitcher with
  glass stirrer
Gin bottle
Fake silver tray
3 martini glasses
2 old-fashioned glasses
3 old-fashioned glasses
1 old-fashioned glass
1 highball glass
Bottle opener
Ice tongs
Cigarette dish

Oil can with water
Toys
Baby carriage
Diapers
Baby bottle
Baby powder
Milk bottle
4 blye wineglasses
1 cup
1 flowered tray
Towel
Shaving cream
Money
2 plastic glasses
Bath towel
Blue folder
Black shoe
Baby spoon
Vacuum cleaner
1 large yellow mug
Blue mug
Empty cornflake box
Plates (2)
Dishcloth
Dish towel
Washcloth
Pots and pans
Electric toothbrush
Perfume bottle
Glass
Briefcase
Umbrella
4 plastic cups
4 plastic saucers
Corkscrew
4 forks
4 tablespoons
4 teaspoons
4 knives
Tureen with ladle
Bottle of white wine,
    corked
Toolbox

Canvas bag with crowbar
Monkey wrench
Dress box
2 dining-room chairs
    (Foster)
2 dining-room chairs
    (Phillips)
2 swivel chairs
Board crash
Tool belt with tools
Trick table
Serving cart
Tray
4 place mats
4 napkins
4 teaspoons
4 forks
4 knives
4 wineglasses
3 serving spoons
Wooden tray
4 orange place mats
4 plastic plates
Roll of paper towels
Candy dish
Screwdriver
4 blue-trimmed cups
    and saucers
Bottle of wine
Round tray
4 gold-rimmed cups
    and saucers
Cream pitcher
Sugar bowl
4 teaspoons
5 cans of beer
Coffeepot
2 cups and saucers
2 spoons
Glass
Sugar bowl
Cream pitcher
Paper napkin

2 spoons
Egg cup
Salt and pepper shakers
2 spoons
Tray

4 plates
Shoebrushes
4 plates
Dishes (3)
2 potholders

COSTUME PLOT

FRANK FOSTER:

ACT ONE—*Scene 1:*
  (a) Jogging outfit, sneakers
  (b) Terry cloth robe, socks, slippers
  (c) Shirt, tie, suit, socks, shoes
  (d) Hat, topcoat, umbrella

ACT ONE—*Scene 2:*
  Repeat, Scene 1 (c) and (d)

ACT TWO—*Scene 1:*
  (a) Jogging outfit, sneakers
  (b) Turtleneck, slacks, blazer, shoes, socks

ACT TWO—*Scene 2:*
  Off—Blazer
  On—Cardigan sweater

TERESA PHILLIPS:

ACT ONE—*Scene 1:*
  Robe, pajamas, slippers, apron

ACT ONE—*Scene 2:*
  (a) Long blouse, slacks, shoes
  (b) Lumber jacket

ACT TWO—*Scene 1:*
  (a) Jumper dress, sweater, cape, boots
  (b) Repeat, Act One, Scene 1 (a)

ACT TWO—*Scene 2:*
  Skirt, turtleneck, poncho shawl, boots

BOB PHILLIPS:

ACT ONE—*Scene 1:*
  (a) Undershirt, trousers, slippers, socks
  (b) Shirt, tie (Add)
  (c) Vest (Add)
  (d) Brown loafers (Add)
  (e) Jacket (Add)
  (f) Raincoat (Add)

ACT ONE—*Scene 2:*
  Different suit

Act Two—*Scene 1:*
  (a) Trousers, socks, slippers (bare to the waist)
  (b) Terry cloth shorts, slippers
  (c) Slacks, robe, slippers

Act Two—*Scene 2:*
Turtleneck, slacks, corduroy jacket, loafers

FIONA FOSTER:

Act One—*Scene 1:*
Dressing gown, pajama bottoms, mules

Act One—*Scene 2:*
Pantsuit, shoes

Act Two—*Scene 1:*
  (a) Long suede vest, wool dress, gloves, shoes, scarf, shoulder bag
  (b) White fringe dress
  (c) Beige slacks, orange blouse

Act Two—*Scene 2:*
Yellow blouse, repeat slacks and shoes

MARY DETWEILER:

Act One—*Scene 2:*
Hat, coat, dress, high-heeled shoes, stockings, cardigan sweater, gloves, bag

Act Two—*Scene 1:*
2nd coat, blouse, skirt, flat shoes, stockings

Act Two—*Scene 2:*
Repeat—Act Two, Scene 1

WILLIAM DETWEILER:

Act One—*Scene 2:*
Rain hat, raincoat, suit, shirt, tie, shoes, socks

Act Two—*Scene 1:*
Corduroy slacks, cardigan sweater, shirt, shoes, socks

Act Two—*Scene 2:*
Shirt, crew neck sweater, same slacks and shoes as Act Two, Scene 1

  NOTE: Suit in Act One, Scene 2. Must have duplicate for drying out of the one doused with soup (water).

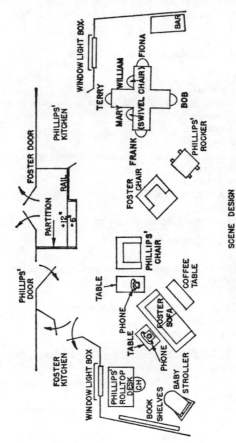

SCENE DESIGN

"HOW THE OTHER HALF LOVES"

110

6 RMS RIV VU
BOB RANDALL
(Little Theatre) Comedy
4 Men, 4 Women, Interior

A vacant apartment with a river view is open for inspection by prospective tenants, and among them are a man and a woman who have never met before. They are the last to leave and, when they get ready to depart, they find that the door is locked and they are shut in. Since they are attractive young people, they find each other interesting and the fact that both are happily married adds to their delight of mutual, yet obviously separate interests.

"... a Broadway comedy of fun and class, as cheerful as a rising souffle. A sprightly, happy comedy of charm and humor. Two people playing out a very vital game of love, an attractive fantasy with a precious tincture of truth to it."—*N.Y. Times.*
"... perfectly charming entertainment, sexy, romantic and funny."—*Women's Wear Daily.*

Royalty, $50—$35

WHO KILLED SANTA CLAUS?
TERENCE FEELY
(All Groups) Thriller
6 Men, 2 Women, Interior

Barbara Love is a popular television 'auntie'. It is Christmas, and a number of men connected with her are coming to a party. Her secretary, Connie, is also there. Before they arrive she is threatened by a disguised voice on her Ansaphone, and is sent a grotesque 'murdered' doll in a coffin, wearing a dress resembling one of her own. She calls the police, and a handsome detective arrives. Shortly afterwards her guests follow. It becomes apparent that one of those guests is planning to kill her. Or is it the strange young man who turns up unexpectedly, claiming to belong to the publicity department, but unknown to any of the others?

"... is a thriller with heaps of suspense, surprises, and nattily cleaver turns and twists ... Mr. Feeley is technically highly skilled in the artificial range of operations, and his dialogue is brilliantly effective."—*The Stage. London.*

Royalty, $50—$25

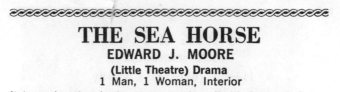

THE SEA HORSE
EDWARD J. MOORE
(Little Theatre) Drama
1 Man, 1 Woman, Interior

It is a play that is, by turns, tender, ribald, funny and suspenseful. Audiences everywhere will take it to their hearts because it is touched with humanity and illuminates with glowing sympathy the complexities of a man-woman relationship. Set in a West Coast waterfront bar, the play is about Harry Bales, a seaman, who, when on shore leave, usually heads for "The Sea Horse," the bar run by Gertrude Blum, the heavy, unsentimental proprietor. Their relationship is purely physical and, as the play begins, they have never confided their private yearnings to each other. But this time Harry has returned with a dream: to buy a charter fishing boat and to have a son by Gertrude. She, in her turn, has made her life one of hard work, by day, and nocturnal love-making; she has encased her heart behind a facade of toughness, utterly devoid of sentimentality, because of a failed marriage. Irwin's play consists in the ritual of "dance" courtship by Harry of Gertrude, as these two outwardly abrasive characters fight, make up, fight again, spin dreams, deflate them, make love and reveal their long locked-up secrets.

"A burst of brilliance!"—*N.Y. Post.* "I was touched close to tears!"—*Village Voice.* "A must! An incredible love story. A beautiful play?"—*Newhouse Newspapers.* "A major new playwright!"—*Variety.*

ROYALTY, $50-$35

THE AU PAIR MAN
HUGH LEONARD
(Little Theatre) Comedy
1 Man, 1 Woman, Interior

The play concerns a rough Irish bill collector named Hartigan, who becomes a love slave and companion to an English lady named Elizabeth, who lives in a cluttered London town house, which looks more like a museum for a British Empire on which the sun has long set. Even the door bell chimes out the national anthem. Hartigan is immediately conscripted into her service in return for which she agrees to teach him how to be a gentleman rather after the fashion of a reverse Pygmalion. The play is a wild one, and is really the never-ending battle between England and Ireland. Produced to critical acclaim at Lincoln Center's Vivian Beaumont Theatre.

ROYALTY, $50-$35